Heaven
in
the
Real
World

Heaven in the Real World

The Transforming Touch of God

Real World

DON MCLAUGHLIN

HOWARD
PUBLISHING CO.

Our purpose at Howard Publishing is:
* *Instructing* believers toward a deeper faith in Jesus Christ
* *Inspiring* holiness in the lives of growing Christians
* *Instilling* hope in the hearts of struggling people everywhere

Because he's coming again

Heaven in the Real World
© 1997 by Howard Publishing Co., Inc.
All rights reserved

Published by Howard Publishing Co., Inc.,
3117 North 7th Street, West Monroe, LA 71291-2227

Printed in the United States of America
Third printing 2001

Cover Design by LinDee Loveland
Edited by Philis Boultinghouse

Library of Congress Cataloging-in-Publication Data

McLaughlin, Don.
    Heaven in the real world : the transforming touch of God / Don McLaughlin.
      p. cm.
    Includes bibliographical references.
    ISBN 1-878990-54-3 (alk. paper)
    1. Christian life. 2. McLaughlin, Don. I. Title.
BV4501.2.M43535 1997
    248.4—dc21   97-684
                                                CIP

DEDICATION

To my wife,
Susan,

our four children,
Don, Aaron, Caleb, and Amy,

the Shepherds of our church family,
Carl, Gene, John, Don, and Scott,

and the faithful staff with whom I share ministry,
Brian and Brad,

all of whom are constant channels of
heaven in my real world.

CONTENTS

PART ONE
Accepting Heaven's Message:
Newness through Relationship

PART TWO
Imitating Heaven's Model:
Impact through Dicscipleship

Contents

PART THREE
Embracing Heaven's Methods:
Maturity through Hardship

Preface

The Inspiration

The opening night of the 1994 Heaven in the Real World concert tour was scheduled for a Thursday in Anderson, Indiana, where I make my home. Due to overwhelming demand and the pull of the alma mater crowd, Steven Curtis Chapman agreed to open Wednesday at Anderson University.

The concert was full of energy and deep with meaning. The beat of the concert was more than music—it reflected the pulse of a generation.

The message of the *Heaven in the Real World* album had a profound impact on my spiritual walk. I began to ask God to openly reveal what it really means for heaven to be in our all-too-real world. Our church felt called by God to make "Heaven in the Real World" our theme for the entire year in 1995.

Preface

God has granted me the opportunity to share his powerful message of presence in our real world all across America at churches, youth conventions, retreats, and university campuses.

Then the Lord moved the hearts of the people at Howard Publishing to make this book possible. Their dedication to making vital resources available to people longing to experience heaven in their real world inspires me when my real world seems dark and my spirit is parched. I thank you all in the name of Jesus Christ. Listen with your heart to the song, "Heaven in the Real World" by Steven Curtis Chapman.

> I saw it again today in the face of a little child
> Looking through eyes of fear and uncertainty
> It echoed in a cry for freedom across the street and
> across the miles
> Cries from the heart to find the missing part
>
> *Chorus:*
> Where is the hope, where is the peace?
> That will make this life complete
> For every man, woman, boy and girl
> Looking for heaven in the real world
>
> To stand in the pouring rain and believe the sun will
> shine again
> To know that the grave is not the end
> To feel the embrace of grace and cross the line where
> real life begins
> And know in your heart you've found the missing
> part

The Inspiration

Chorus:
There is a hope, there is a peace
That will make this life complete
For every man, woman, boy and girl
Looking for heaven in the real world
Heaven in the real world

Bridge:
It happened one night with a tiny baby's birth
God heard creation crying and
He sent heaven to earth

Chorus:
He is the hope, He is the peace
That will make this life complete
For every man, woman, boy and girl
Looking for heaven in the real world

He is the hope, He is the peace
That will make this life complete
For every man, woman, boy and girl
Looking for heaven in the real world
Heaven has come to the real world
Heaven has come, come to the real world
He is the hope, He is the peace
Jesus is heaven, heaven in the real world
He is the hope
He is heaven in the real world
He is the peace
He is heaven in the real world[1]

ACKNOWLEDGMENTS

God the eternal is my faith anchor. Jesus the Savior is the original from whom, in whom, and to whom are all things. The Holy Spirit, God with his sleeves rolled up, is the patient transformer of my life into his dwelling. To you, I offer the life you gave me.

I thank my dad and mom for blazing the trail of faithfulness to God and setting the pace for commitment to reading and writing. I thank my wife and children who bring so much of God's will to human form. Thanks to Susan's parents, Walt and Shirley McIndoo for making "family" come alive.

I thank Byron Fike for telling me the story of Jesus, and Jerry Jones for modeling the story for me. Thanks to Gloria Gaither for imprinting my first effort with her grace and experience. Thanks to Steven Curtis Chapman and all Christian musicians who pierce our hearts with the message through song. Thanks to all the churches who have sponsored retreats, youth rallies, meetings, and workshops in which these thoughts were allowed a hearing.

Acknowledgments

Thanks to the shepherds, staff, and family of the Lindberg Road church in Anderson, Indiana, for all their love, support, and sharpening. Thanks to my home Bible study group for sharing with us and carrying us. Thanks to Jeff, Harper, and my friends in Morgantown, West Virginia for all the assistance in reading, critiquing, and preparing of the manuscript. Thanks to Gary, Kristen, Gabriel, Hannah, and Samara Myers, and Kirby, Annie, Amy, and Kristen Graham for being friends that stick closer than a brother. Thanks to Howard Publishing for bringing this book from opportunity to reality. A very special thanks to Philis Boultinghouse for editing out my ramblings and editing in the clarity of the message of Christ.

Introduction

"Dear Dad, Please don't die."

I received this plea in a homemade get well card in May of 1992 from my eight-year-old son. Two weeks earlier my left knee had been reconstructed following the discovery that volleyball with college students is a full-contact sport. A sports injury at the age of thirty-two is kind of cool. I mean, it's better than falling down the stairs, and it gives you an excuse for being a little slower out there on the playing field.

But the surgery was not the end. The following week was a living nightmare. I began feeling sick and running a fever. Every joint in my body was filled with the kind of pain I could only liken to the throbbing of a finger smashed by a hammer. Finally, in the midst of delirious pain, a close

1

friend and my wife, Susan, rushed me to the emergency room of our local hospital. After four hours of X-rays, morphine, and frantic phone calls to specialists, they told me I was being taken to a larger hospital in Indianapolis, where I would have emergency surgery to remove infection from my knee.

Infection? Too sick to care and in too much pain to think, I faded in and out of consciousness during the forty-minute ambulance dash to Indy. The doctor was waiting at the emergency room. It was 6:40 A.M. on a Saturday morning. He said, "We're going to take you to surgery right now and do our best to save this knee."

A sports injury at the age of thirty-two is kind of cool. I mean, it's better than falling down the stairs, and it gives you an excuse for being a little slower out there on the playing field.

I didn't care at that point what they did, but I did say, "Whatever happens, tell it to me straight. I'm a minister, and I see this from the other side all the time. Don't tell my wife anything you don't tell me, and don't tell me anything you're not going to tell her." He shook his head in agreement, and that's the last I remember of that day.

When I awakened the following Sunday morning, my already poor eyesight was blurred even more by the anesthesia. I looked at the bloody wrapping on my left knee, but because of the angle and the

Demerol, I couldn't see or feel my left leg from the knee down.

At least I'm alive, I thought. *I can handle losing a leg. Thank God, he spared my life.*

"My name is Doctor Buntz."

Although he must have thought I was awake, his announcement called me from slumber. I stirred and tried to focus on the doctor standing at the foot of my bed.

"I am an infection specialist," he said, "and I understand from the surgeon that you want to hear the news straight out."

Although I wasn't too focused up to this point and was trying to figure out why the orthopedic surgeon had been replaced by an infection specialist, his last phrase riveted my attention on his words.

"Yes, I do want it straight," I stammered.

"You have a systemic staph infection in your blood. Your blood is like a river of poison releasing deadly toxins in your entire system all at the same time. You are in the advanced stages. If we can't arrest this in the next twenty-four to forty-eight hours, you'll die."

I remember thinking, *I didn't want it that straight!*

I looked at him and just said, "What?"

He gave me a quizzical look like, *Did I stutter? I said you're going to die.*

He continued very matter of factly, "We have already put you on Vancomyacin, the second most powerful antibiotic available. It will either kill you or save you, but you have nothing to lose and everything to gain. We don't know how long this will take, but we will do our best. Do you have any questions?"

At that point I thought, *I've got questions, but they're not the kind you can answer.* As he left, he turned and said, "You appear to be a fighter. If you have ever waited for a moment to fight for all your worth, that moment has arrived!"

I thought, *I am a fighter, and I will beat this thing!*

It was now 9:00 A.M. In three more hours Susan would be at my side asking what the doctor had said. What would I tell her? When she arrived, I simply parroted exactly what the doctor had told me. Susan looked me straight in the eye, fighting back the tears, and said, "You are not going to die and leave me with four kids!"

Fortified by her statement of solidarity and courage, I now thought, *We will beat this thing.* The determination I felt that morning quickly faded into the ravaging realities of the infection. My situation steadily worsened over the next few days as my body fought back against the overwhelming enemy invaders. Unable to eat, drink, or even get out of bed, I lost twenty-seven pounds (that I didn't have to lose), and I looked like an extra for *Return of the Zombies.*

Then came the card from Bub. All four of our young children entered my hospital room, seeing me for the first time in six days. Although I tried to look strong for them, I could tell that the sight of me was more than Susan had been able to prepare them for. Quietly, they made their way to my bed. Curiosity at all the beeping machines, dripping tubes, and blinking screens distracted them from their fears.

My skin crawled with the longing to touch them. My soul hungered for their nearness. Somehow, Susan got them all on the hospital bed, and one at a time I felt their little arms searching for some part of me to hold. They felt the same longing for nearness that I did.

Then Bub (our nickname for my namesake), the oldest, handed me his card. The message was simple, direct, and powerful: *"Dear Dad, Please don't die."*

His request set off an emotional bomb inside of me, and a flood of realization poured over me. Even though *I* was willing to fight for all I was worth, even though *Susan* had declared that I was not going to die, even though the *kids* wanted me to live—I realized that even all of this together was not enough. I couldn't save myself, nor could all of my loving relationships. If I was to live, I would need a power greater than this earth could offer. If I was going to die, I would need the power of heaven to face that reality. Obviously, the Lord chose to keep me here for a while longer.

I'm guessing that right now you are living a story of your own. As a counselor and minister for the past fourteen years, I have been stunned, grieved, shocked, and horrified at the suffering I've seen people endure. Maybe you are struggling with disease, divorce, downsizing, abuse, or impending death. Or perhaps you are burdened with the daily grind of straining every nerve simply to survive in a going-nowhere-anytime-soon life.

As I have heard people describe their painful existence as a "living hell," I have often wondered, Why does earth seem like hell for children of heaven? Does it have to be this way? Or is God willing and able to bring his power to bear on our lives right now so that we can experience heaven in our real world?

In the pages of this book, I will share real-life stories of people just like you and me—people who saw no way out until they looked up. I will also share the Monday-through-Friday biblical principles that served as guiding lights for these people in the dark tunnels of their suffering. My prayer is that this book will lead you to a fuller experience of the power of heaven in your daily life. In a word, this book is about *power*—transforming power. Not the personal power of a self-help regimen, but the power of heaven to influence life in your daily world. This power will enable you to live a life you won't want to quit, to build relationships you won't want to leave, to weather difficulties without being washed away by the storm, and to serve a purpose higher than any earthly cause.

Heaven in the Real World is about how the power of God can influence the way you face each situation in your daily life—great or small.

Living within the power of God sounds exciting and enticing, but such a life does not come with the flip of a spiritual light switch. His power to drastically improve the quality of your everyday life is not "just a prayer away"—as some would have you believe. Allowing the power of God to influence your life requires more than an occasional last-ditch-effort prayer. It demands your mind, your will, your time, and your energy. Being carried by the power of God means learning new ways of thinking, feeling, acting, and communicating. In short, living in the power of God means submitting your life to the influence of heaven.

This book is divided into three sections. Section one explores the power of God's *message of enlightenment*. We live in the information age, yet so little accurate information is disseminated about God. There is an incredible surge of confidence that comes from accepting what God reveals about himself, about heaven, and about his true feelings and dreams for us.

The second section is devoted to the power of imitating the *model of heaven* in the life of Jesus Christ. Giving *attention* to God's Word and expressing *appreciation* to God are not enough. We must go one step farther—we must learn to experience the *power* of God by living out the life of Christ on a daily

In a word, this book is about power.

basis. There is no substitute for consciously imitating the example of the most influential man who ever lived.

The final section is required reading for those of us who need to learn how to appreciate God's *methods for maturing us*. Our world rarely equates love with difficulty or delay, and when we encounter these on our journey of faith, we often feel frustrated with God. Tragedies, the presence of evil, seemingly unanswered prayers, and the hypocritical lives of those professing faith can all mask the true face of heaven. The principles in the third section of this book will help you reshape your view of the hardships encountered on your journey of faith.

You and I are making this journey of faith together. In fact, we join millions of fellow travelers. God told Abraham to "look to the *heavens*,"[1] and Paul declared "I press on toward the goal to win the prize for which God has called me *heavenward* in Christ Jesus."[2] If you, like me, want your life to take on new meaning, significance, and power, then set your sights heavenward and use this book as your launching pad.

Accepting Heaven's Message

Newness through Relationship

Part One Prelude

How dare he say that they had "never heard [God's] voice"![1]

The Jews diligently studied the Scriptures. They had literally thousands of pages of commentary on God's laws in their Talmud and Mishna. How could anyone, least of all a carpenter from Nazareth, level such a scathing indictment?

Nevertheless, he did. Jesus knew there was a difference between reading the Scriptures and actually hearing the voice of God through the Scriptures.

Accepting heaven's message means allowing heaven to speak for itself. Too often, we interpret heaven's message through our own life experiences, or we allow others—human teachers, traditions, television, etc.—to interpret heaven for us. But if we would only allow heaven to speak for itself, we would hear a message that would thrill our souls and satisfy our innermost longings. For at the heart of God's message for you are two things that every person desires—a *fresh start* and a *meaningful relationship.*

I ask one commitment of you before you turn the page: *Let God speak for himself.* Hear *his* voice and not the voice of human distracters. If heaven is to enter your real world and vitally change your life, you must hear its message accurately, "for faith comes from hearing the message, and the message is heard through the word of Christ."[2]

1

Heaven's Priority

Restoring Your Value

Our family rarely goes out for a sit-down dinner. Since there are six of us, eating out often could spawn fiscal disaster. But one Sunday evening, Susan and the children prevailed upon me to dine out at the Cracker Barrel restaurant.

Following a good meal and a great time together, we drove back by the church building. Due to schedules and ministries we are involved in, we often drive two vehicles, so we stopped to pick up my four-wheel-drive Blazer. It was a hot and sticky summer night—about 9 P.M. Since my truck had no air conditioning, I drove home with the windows down. Susan and the kids followed in the van.

About two miles from our home, I heard an agonizing scream. Instinctively, I looked in my left rear-view mirror to catch some visible explanation. At first I saw just my family in our van, but after we both passed the point of the scream, I was horrified to see a young, muscular man dragging a woman across the street by her hair. He was hitting her so hard with his fist that nearly every punch lifted her writhing body off the ground.

Susan and the kids did not hear the scream since their windows were closed, but when I slammed on the brakes and pulled a U-turn in the road, they followed. I drove right up into the front yard of a house across the street from where I first spotted the man and woman. I honked the horn and flashed the bright lights. Startled, the man dropped the battered woman and ran out of sight into the darkness. She began to stagger toward the truck.

> He was hitting her so hard with his fist that nearly every punch lifted her writhing body off the ground.

Fearing his return and concerned about her condition, I called out to her, "I know you don't know us, but we are safe. Please get in the truck, and we'll help you." She made her way into the front seat, and as I began to drive out of the yard, she covered her face with her hands. Each time she coughed, her body convulsed from the pain of the pummeling.

"Can I take you to the hospital, or home?" I stammered.

"Please just take me to my parents' house around the block."

We drove in silence for a few moments until we arrived at the rear of their property in an alley. I ran back to brief Susan and told her to notify the police. Sherry (not her real name) began limping along the narrow concrete walkway to the back door. She stopped a few times to cough up blood. I was frightened for her.

Her mom and dad opened the back door. The parental terror on their faces, reflected in the dim porch light, broke my heart. Sherry's mother quickly but tenderly embraced her and escorted her to the kitchen sink to begin cleaning the wounds.

Her father, a large and fit man of about fifty, bent down and began to lace up his work boots. Envisioning his destination, I gently prodded, "Where are you going?"

His answer made a deep impression on me: "I told him *last time this happened* that I would handle it my own way if it ever happened again!"

Last time? I thought. *This has happened before? This shouldn't happen even once to anyone.*

I told him that we had already notified the police, and I pleaded with him to stay here—where his daughter needed him. We both went over and sat down under the fluorescent light at a small chrome and Formica kitchen table. He wept externally and I internally. He recounted five years of abuse Sherry had suffered at the hands of her boyfriend, beginning in high school. Although they never married, she had continued her relationship with this convicted, jailed, and released abuser.

When Sherry finally turned into the light, I tried to hide my shock at what I saw. Because of the darkness, I had not seen the extent of her injuries. Her eyes were completely swollen shut, and her face was beaten beyond recognition. She needed immediate hospital care. They wanted to go privately, so we said a brief prayer, left our phone number, and drove home.

Our children were remarkably reverent as we readied for bed and prayed for Sherry and her family. The following morning we sent Sherry and her family flowers with a note penned by my wife which read, "Just a note to let you know others care when your family hurts."

Although we prayed for them often, we did not hear from them for ten months. Then one afternoon the following spring, I joined one of the men from our church for lunch at a favorite local restaurant. We were barely seated at our table when a bright, vibrant young waitress walked straight over to our table, looked right at me with a definite sparkle in her eyes, and said, "Do you remember me?"

For a split second I was unsure, but then I knew. I felt so many emotions, and my eyes began to well up with tears.

"Yes, Sherry, I remember you. Please sit down."

With a strong and clear voice she shared, "I just want to thank you and your family for what you did that night last summer. You were all so brave. It was so much worse than ever before; I thought he would kill me. So many others just drove on, even when we were near the street."

I was embarrassed by her statements and momentarily interrupted, "I'm no hero, Sherry; we just did what God has shown us. Besides, I was just going to run over him if I had to. I'm not the brave one."

She continued, "Later that night I thought about my whole life in a new light. If someone who didn't even know me cared enough to risk his life to help me, I must be more special than I had ever realized. I moved back in with my parents the next day, started back to college, landed this good job, and have never seen him again. I am prosecuting— for everyone's best good."

Both my friend and I were openly shedding tears at her testimony. I could barely choke out my feelings.

"Sherry, you are the one with courage! You are the hero. Out of the thousands of abused people, only a fraction are willing to be permanently rescued; only a few will be brave enough to face the changes a new life requires."

What was it that changed Sherry's view of herself? It was seeing herself through the eyes of *someone else*. Until then, she had seen herself through untrained eyes. She was like the person who merely glances at valuable pieces of art in an art gallery. But when the expert guide comes along and explains the immense uniqueness and value of each work, they are henceforth and forever viewed as the priceless masterpieces they are. And because someone else had seen her worth, Sherry now saw it too.

God is desperate for us to see his view of us. He wants to overpower or even eradicate the view we have of ourselves—a view that is the result of Satan's constant chipping away at our self-image and self-value.

Accepting heaven's message begins with understanding God's priority of intimacy. One of the most important sections of Scripture describing heaven in the real world is Matthew 13, which contains the parables of the kingdom.

The thread of continuity through the parables powerfully reveals God's view of us. The opening parable about the different soils shows us God's willingness to go into the field, which is the world. He himself is the farmer. He is his own missionary. He is a blue-collar God who pursues closeness to all people, three-fourths of whom, according to the parable, will either not make a commitment to him or will ultimately break any commitment they make. He pursues and plants nevertheless.

In the parable of the weeds and the net, God presents himself as one who is even willing to allow the wicked to remain in the presence of the righteous, all the way to the very end. Why? God does not want to accidentally injure the righteous in the purge of the wicked, and he "is patient with you, not wanting anyone to perish, but everyone to come to repentance."[1]

Then in verse 44 he paints a picture of his heart in one broad stroke. Read carefully, noting that he has already defined the field as the world and himself as the man in the field: "The kingdom of heaven is like a treasure hidden in a field. When a man found it, he hid it again, and then in his joy went and sold all he had and bought that field."[2]

What is heaven like? Heaven is like God coming into the world, finding a hidden treasure, and selling everything he has to obtain the treasure. And what is this valuable treasure he is willing to give up all to gain? *You and me!*

Intimacy with you is top priority with God. Candidly, God can't get over you. Even when you frustrate his every effort to show his love, his passion for you is undiminished. His love for you *is* the divine romance.

God's priority of nearness changes how we view ourselves and others—just as Sherry's view of herself changed, when she saw herself through the eyes of others. The fact that we are treasured by God raises our value. God knew this elevation of value would change the way we live—just like Sherry's realization of her value changed the way she lived—so he made it heaven's priority to demonstrate his desire for closeness this side of eternity.

Beginning in the Garden, God desired nearness with Adam and Eve. In its pristine state, God actually walked in the Garden—he was close to his creation. And ever since the Fall, God has worked to restore that intimacy.

The book of Deuteronomy speaks of God's nearness to his people, "What other nation is so great as to have their gods near them the way the Lord our God is near us?"[3] And the book of James promises that if we will come near to God, he will come near to us.[4]

> Believing that we are cherished and held close to his heart will transform us and empower us to live on an infinitely higher plain.

The description of our salvation in Ephesians 2:6 further demonstrates God's priority of nearness. We are described as "raised up with Christ and seated with him in the heavenly realms." Notice carefully and joyfully that the verbs in that sentence are in the *past tense*. In God's mind, we are already citizens of heaven, shoulder to shoulder and hip to hip with him—even now![5]

Why does God want you and me to be convinced that he loves being close to us? Because believing that we are cherished and held close to his heart will transform us and empower us to live on an infinitely higher plain.

Everything God does centers in his eternal desire to be close to you. Remember this foundation. It is crucial. God declares that you are treasured! "And the Lord has declared this day that you are his people, his *treasured* possession."[6] Even if you choose to reject him through unbelief or rebellion, you cannot quench his fire for you.

Take a few moments to meditate on the words of the following song—"Treasure of You"—by Steven Curtis Chapman and Geoff Moore. Then at least commit to learning more about this God who *cares* about you, *loves* you, and *treasures* you.

> Excuse Me, I couldn't help but notice
> That heartsick look in your eyes.
> You hide it very well, but I've got the same disguise.
> I know, from all you see around you,
> You feel worth a very small price,
> So plain and ordinary, but there's a pearl inside.
> And if you look in the mirror, in the light of the
>   truth,
> You'll see there's really nothing you could say or do,
> To make you worth more to the one who made you.
>
> The rich man treasures gold and silver,
> The wise man, his knowledge of truth.
> Some will hold to memories,
>   and some will cling to youth.

But to the one who carved out the oceans,
And painted the stars in the sky,
You are His prized creation—the apple of His eye.
There's no one else in the world
    who could take your place.
Just the thought of you brings a smile to his face.
God loves you with amazing grace.

God made everything, and of everything He made,
More than anything He treasures you and me.
Check it in the mirror in the light of the truth,
There is nothing you will ever say,
    and nothing you will do,
That will ever make God care more
    than He does for the treasure.
God's treasure is you.

Chorus:
You are a treasure,
Worth more than anything under the sun or the
    moon.
God's greatest treasure
Is the treasure of you,
The treasure of you.[7]

2

Heaven's Provision

Offering Total Pardon

On a dark night in 1982, a policeman in Indiana was dispatched to check out a traffic accident reported to have occurred in his neighborhood. As the patrol car headlights illuminated the scene, steam from a demolished vehicle rose above the shadows of the gathering crowd. One victim, a teenage girl, was dead at the steering wheel. Her passenger, now lying prone on the pavement in a pool of blood, died later at the hospital.

Up in a yard bordering the intersection was a young man sitting with his back against his wrecked pickup. As the officer approached the boy, whose face was buried in his hands, he could hear him sobbing. Laying his hand on the boy's shoulder, the officer could smell liquor. The boy was sobbing the same phrase repeatedly, "I didn't mean to do it. I didn't mean to do it."

After leaving an unsupervised party that included under-age drinking, he was unable to respond to the stop sign at the intersection. He slammed into the girls' car at nearly eighty miles per hour, and they never knew what hit them. The two deaths rocked the small town; but their emotions would have to endure one more tragedy. As the intoxication wore off and the guilt wore on, the young man was overwhelmed with his responsibility in the death of two innocent victims. The day he was released from the hospital, one week after the accident, he took his own life.

> The boy was sobbing the same phrase repeatedly, "I didn't mean to do it. I didn't mean to do it."

He saw no way out. The debt he owed was beyond payment. There was nothing he could do to bring the girls back or replace them. His only hope for life after their death was pardon, but he didn't seek it. He was sure it was not available.

Seven years later, in August of 1989, I got a call from a doctor in our church. He summoned me to the hospital to help with a family. He had been in emergency surgery all night, working on a man who was barely alive after a severe accident. I asked what happened, and the situation was nearly a carbon copy of the first accident I described.

The man, in his thirties, had left a bar quite intoxicated. Crossing the center line on a rural road, he struck a car with two female passengers head on. Both women were killed. I met him that day at the hospital. His grief was immense and only increased as time went on.

The ending of his story, however, is quite different. Although he still grieves the accident and did go to prison for his crime, he appealed to God for pardon. In November of 1989, he confessed his need for Christ to cleanse his conscience and became a Christian. He found forgiveness and pardon.

These twin situations had completely different endings.

A similar situation is reflected in the apostles Peter and Judas Iscariot. Peter denied, and Judas betrayed. There is very little difference between the two offenses. Both men were bitterly sorry. But Peter lived to preach the first sermon on Pentecost, and Judas killed himself. The difference was pardon.

Peter accepted the pardon that was available to him, and Judas did not. We don't know all the reasons one man was able to receive God's pardon and one was not, but perhaps part of the answer lies in an earlier exchange between Peter and Jesus. Perhaps the lessons that Peter learned during this discussion helped him in the dark hours following his denial of Christ.

> Peter came to Jesus and asked, "Lord, how many times shall I forgive my brother when he sins against me? Up to seven times?"
>
> Jesus answered, "I tell you not seven times, but seventy-seven times.

"Therefore, the kingdom of heaven is like a king who wanted to settle accounts with his servants. As he began the settlement, a man who owed him ten thousand talents was brought to him. Since he was not able to pay, the master ordered that he and his wife and his children and all that he had be sold to repay the debt.

"The servant fell on his knees before him. 'Be patient with me,' he begged, 'and I will pay back everything.' The servant's master took pity on him, canceled the debt, and let him go.

"But when that servant went out, he found one of his fellow servants who owed him a hundred denarii. He grabbed him and began to choke him. 'Pay back what you owe me!' he demanded.

"His fellow servant fell to his knees and begged him, 'Be patient with me, and I will pay you back.'

"But he refused. Instead, he went off and had the man thrown into prison until he could pay the debt. When the other servants saw what had happened, they were greatly distressed and went and told their master everything that had happened.

"Then the master called the servant in. 'You wicked servant,' he said, 'I canceled all that debt of yours because you begged me to. Shouldn't you have had mercy on your fellow servant just as I had on you?' In anger his master turned him over to the jailers to be tortured, until he should pay back all he owed.

"This is how my heavenly Father will treat each of you unless you forgive your brother from your heart."[1]

Peter learned much about pardon from this parable, and so can we. Jesus begins this teaching with a notice: *Here is what heaven is like in regard to dealing with sin.* Jesus tells us what he's going to tell us so we won't miss the message, but many miss it anyway. Too often people take the liberty of speaking for God, and quite inaccurately! I often hear people say, "God will never forgive me for this or that." This is exactly the fatal thinking of Judas and the young boy I mentioned earlier. Jesus tells a different story.

There are four key points about the pardon of heaven in this parable.

1. Sin does not go unnoticed. The king did and will settle accounts. You and I are accountable to God for the way we live. Jesus says we will give an account of ourselves to God on the Day of Judgment. The apostle Paul echoes this teaching: "So then, each of us will give an account of himself to God."[2]

The Hebrew writer drives home this same doctrine of accountability before God: "Nothing in all creation is hidden from God's sight. Everything is uncovered and laid bare before the eyes of him to whom we must give account."[3]

2. The debt we owe is beyond payment. The man in the parable owed millions. One commentator/historian suggested that if the ten thousand talents he owed was due in gold, he owed more than a year's national taxes that the entire country of Israel would pay to Rome. Whether or not this math is exactly correct, the reason Jesus used such an exorbitant amount was to emphasize the point that the man owed far more than he could pay. Our debt, too, is beyond payment. But our debt is related to sin, not money; and the consequence is hell, not prison. Left to our own resources, we are doomed.

3. *Pardon is our only hope.* Without the pardon of the king, the man would have rotted in prison, with no chance to pay the debt. Without pardon, we will spend eternity in hell. We have nothing to offer in payment for our grave debt. Pardon is our only hope. Why was the king willing to forgive the debt? Because he wanted to. His servant was more important to him than what his servant owed him. The king hoped that by releasing the debt he would receive the servant as a grateful friend.

> Heaven's priority of intimacy is the driving force behind heaven's pardon.

4. *We must choose to receive the pardon.* The terrible actions of the selfish servant proved that he did not receive the pardon as the king had given it. Please notice a subtle indicator to this character flaw in the servant. He didn't actually ask for pardon—he asked for *patience*—which indicates that he thought he could pay his own debt. The fact that he thought he could handle the debt himself cheapened the grace of the king. In fact, the man acted as if the king's mercy was really unnecessary.

Since he didn't truly "receive" in his heart the pardon given by the king, he didn't experience the transforming power of heaven's pardon. When he met up with his fellow servant, he was still his ugly, unconverted self. In actuality, he still owed the full debt to the king, because he never appropriated the pardon. This is why the king eventually jailed him. It is also why Jesus told the Jews, and us, that if we don't forgive others, we will receive the full wrath of heaven.

But God's desire for us is *not* that we suffer his eternal wrath—his desire is to share eternal *intimacy* with us. Yes, our sin is a barrier to intimacy, but this truth does not diminish his desire for closeness. His love for us drives him to overcome that barrier. Heaven's priority of intimacy is the driving force behind heaven's pardon.

Make no mistake about it. Our debt was taken into account. The full amount was paid. No breaks were given. No discounts offered. No preferential passes on punishment were allowed. Jesus suffered insults because of our immorality. He was drenched in spit for our spite. He was slapped for our selfishness, punched for our pettiness, crowned with thorns for our cruel threats, and murdered for our malice. He was crucified for our callousness.

Our sin—yours and mine—was not easily atoned. Our pardon was purchased at great cost. But it was purchased! And now it is ours for the taking. It is full and free and sufficient! Jesus Christ is the atoning sacrifice for our sins. Because of him, we can live and not die.

In chapter one, we discussed heaven's message of *value*. The message of *pardon* is the second message we must accept if we are to experience the transforming power of heaven in the real world of our guilt. Before you take another step, appeal to the king of heaven for a full pardon. In one glorious moment, you can be totally absolved of all your sin. No conditions.

If you are coming to this for the first time, read Acts 2:1–47 and simply follow what you find. If you are coming back to God for the thousandth time, for the same sin, read 1 John 1:5–2:6 and embrace the grace. If you're like the unpardoned servant, you're still only a step away. Take an inventory of your relationships. If there is one person you have not forgiven, take the name to the throne of God in prayer. Ask God to teach you how to forgive that person. Search his Word for examples of forgiveness; get help from a mature and objective Christian.

> Jesus was drenched in spit for our spite. He was slapped for our selfishness, punched for our pettiness, crowned with thorns for our cruel threats, and murdered for our malice.

Then ask God to pardon you. Confess to him that you can't ever stop sinning—let alone pay for the sins you've already committed. Look closely at the marred and battered body of Jesus. Your sins are the signatures on every wound. Look into his forgiving eyes and cry for mercy. Get close enough to the Cross that you can feel his blood sprinkle your heart and cleanse it. You are released from your debt. You are free! Free to free others and bring the pardon of heaven to their real world, free to experience the transforming power of pardon in your own life and know intimacy with God.

3

Heaven's Purpose

Transforming Our Image

The storm had been vicious and unrelenting. Cleanup would be arduous and depressing. The lost explorer lamented to himself, "Maybe even rescue isn't worth the pain of survival in this God-forsaken place."

A decade earlier this young indomitable explorer had jumped at the challenge of navigating this uncharted terrain of deep canyons, towering mountains, and dense forests. The exhilaration of man against the elements and the conquest of insurmountable peaks made the explorer feel invincible.

Then came the fall. Safety ropes had long since been discarded as a nuisance, and an irresponsible self-confidence had replaced respect for the silent sovereignty of gravity. Loosing his grip, the invincible man crashed to the canyon floor and was knocked unconscious. Although he regained his senses, the fall left his body battered, his confidence tattered, and his supplies scattered. He was lost in this unforgiving maze of look-a-like canyons and mirror-image mountains without a compass, map, or survival kit.

And now, after ten years of battling the elements, this last storm eroded more than the soil.

And now, after ten years of battling the elements, this last storm eroded more than the soil. His depression intensified.

Outside his makeshift hut of mud, stone, and branches, the rain had finally stopped. The only sound was the rhythmic procession of water drops making their way leaf by leaf to the canyon floor. The stillness marked the end of the fiercest storm ever to pound its way through this valley of despair.

Pushing back the old rain poncho now serving as a door, he saw debris strewn all across the small plot of flat ground in front of his little hut. The once smooth surface was now eroded like a plowed field. One small puddle of muddy water, however, seemed especially bright, like something other than the water was reflecting the sun's rays. Kneeling at the shallow pool, he could see a cloudy reflection beneath the surface. His fingers dipped below the surface to find that the object uncovered by the erosion had a smooth, glass-like surface.

He quickly brushed away the mud and silt to find the edges. Then, pulling with all his might until the tips of his fingers burned, the suction gave way and the piece came up in his hands. Shining like the sun and about the size of a silver serving tray, it was a beautiful brass shield—apparently lost many years ago by some ancient warrior.

As he carefully scanned its intricate designs, he was suddenly startled by something he hadn't seen in ten years—his own reflection. It was hazy at best, but it was him. He immediately dropped to one knee and began to brush and clean the mirror feverishly. With all his might he polished the shield into a beautiful mirror. Finally, the moment came when he grasped the shield, now a mirror, held it firmly at arms length, and fixed his gaze on the image reflected in the mirror.

He blinked, squinted, and repositioned the mirror at several angles. Nothing helped the reflection. He looked awful! His hair was straggly and his eyes were bloodshot. Dirt-smeared wrinkles lined his weathered face, and his entire body was scarred from the fall. Could this be his true reflection? His intense stare turned into an angry glare.

"This can't possibly be me," he muttered. But the more he polished the mirror, the more lucid the reflection became. In his anger he threw the shield to the ground and began to stone it. "Never has any man encountered such an evil and deceitful mirror, and never will he again," he said, as he continued to bury the shield under the growing mound of rocks. Eventually, the pile grew into a small mountain. Finally, he took his rest on top of the mound. He was victorious over the mirror, yet helpless to improve his condition.

And to add to his dirt, weariness, and scars, he was now filled with bitterness.

Instead of affirming his strength and applauding his self-made status, the mirror had starkly revealed his deplorable condition.

The explorer in this parable is you and me, and the mirror is the Word of God. Many of us have confidently set out to "explore life for ourselves." And then when life's storms and falls finally bring us face to face with the mirror of God's Word, we look into it longingly, hoping to see a reflection of our own goodness and completeness before God. Instead, the image we see is one of a scarred, dirty, unkempt soul. And to complicate matters even more, we see a second reflection in the mirror—the reflection of a holy and just God—a God who is wholly different from ourselves. Compared to him, our hopeless state is even more evident.

And we become angry with the mirror, and in disappointment, we cast it aside, claiming that any flaws in our reflection are actually defects in the mirror. We begin covering the mirror with stones of philosophy and criticism, and we accuse those who extol it of shallowness and hypocrisy. We sit firmly on the mound of bitterness—still scarred, still scattered, still hurt.

As long as we see the reflection as our judgment, we will be frustrated by the seemingly brutal honesty of the mirror. If all we see is ourselves and our poor reflection of the holiness of God, the mirror just makes us hopelessly aware that we are sinners. But if we can see the reflection as a guidance system to help us transform our image, we will find hope for our own future, and we will find joy in the reflection of God as creator, lover, savior, father, and friend. And as our understanding increases, we will learn to see the reflection of our image as a means of knowing what in us needs changing—what needs *transforming*.

The first step in our transformation is extreme. The first step is our own *death*. In Romans 6, Paul said, "All of us who were baptized into Christ Jesus were baptized into his *death*. . . . Our old self was *crucified* with him so that the body of sin might be done away with."[1] In order to be transformed into the image of Christ, we must first die. But Paul goes on to say that "if we have been united with [Christ] like this in his death, we will certainly also be united with him in his resurrection."[2]

And now that we are raised with Christ, our whole way of thinking is changed.

> We become angry with the mirror, and in our disappointment, we cast it aside, claiming that any flaws in our reflection are actually defects in the mirror.

Since, then, you have been raised with Christ, set your hearts on things above, where Christ is seated at the right hand of God. Set your minds on things above, not on earthly things. For you died, and your life is now hidden with Christ in God.[3]

In essence, Paul is saying that our entire identity has changed and that now we are to live like pardoned people who share heaven's purpose.

The Bible also talks about our transformation in terms of *clothing*. The parable of the wedding banquet, recorded in Matthew 22 reveals the importance of being clothed with Christ.

> The kingdom of heaven is like a king who prepared a wedding banquet for his son. He sent his servants to tell them to come, but they refused to come....
>
> Then he said to his servants, "The wedding banquet is ready, but those I invited did not deserve to come. Go to the street corners and invite to the banquet anyone you find." So the servants went out into the streets and gathered all the people they could find, both good and bad, and the wedding hall was filled with guests.
>
> But when the king came in to see the guests, he noticed a man there who was not wearing the wedding clothes. "Friend," he asked, "how did you get in here without wedding clothes?" The man was speechless.
>
> Then the king told the attendants, "Tie him hand and foot, and throw him outside, into the darkness, where there will be weeping and gnashing of teeth."
>
> For many are invited, but few are chosen.[4]

Talk about a bummer! This guy goes to a wedding he didn't even know about twenty-four hours earlier, and he gets canned for not wearing the right clothes. Doesn't this seem a bit unfair?

But there is so much more to the situation than meets the eye. The custom, as evidenced in the passage, was that the master of the wedding banquet provided wedding clothes for everyone who attended. The reason the man was speechless is that he had no defense. Had he no wedding clothes available, the argument would be simple and justified. But since the clothes were presented to him free of charge, he had to have some darker reason for rejecting the garments. The master of the banquet was aware of the man's evil motive and did not allow him to even finish the meal.

God's grace provides us with the righteous robe of Christ, allowing us to come to the banquet. This is our *initial* transformation. And then heaven works in our lives in a process of *continual* transformation. See what Paul has to say about the transforming power of our "clothing."

> As God's chosen people, holy and dearly loved, *clothe* yourselves with compassion, kindness, humility, gentleness and patience.[5]

> *Clothe* yourselves with the Lord Jesus Christ, and do not think about how to gratify the desires of the sinful nature.[6]

> Rid yourselves of all such things as these: anger, rage, malice, slander, and filthy language from your lips. Do not lie to each other since you have *taken off* your old self with its practices and have *put on* your new self, which is *being renewed* in knowledge in the image of its Creator.[7]

Heaven's message of transformation has its roots in the Garden of Eden with the first couple. God created Adam and Eve in his perfect image, but they were soon seduced by Satan and fell. In an attempt to remedy their situation, they made clothes for themselves. "Then the eyes of both of them were opened, and they realized they were naked; so they sewed fig leaves together and made coverings for them-selves."[8]

Adam and Eve had violated the intimate relationship they had with God, and then they attempted to regain what was lost through their own efforts.

This pattern is still played out today. We turn from the image in which we are created, and then we try to figure out ways to reclothe ourselves on our own. This earthly clothing comes in the form of money, success, popularity, and especially religious goodness. It's true that these articles of human clothing have the appearance of fulfilling our needs, but there is no real substance or power in them.[9]

When God comes to redeem us, he asks us the same question he asked Adam, "Where are you?"[10] He doesn't ask that question for his own good, but for ours. He is not lost, we are. When the master of the banquet approached the man who was inappropriately dressed, he asked him, "How did you get in here without wedding clothes?" The answer was not for the benefit of the master, but to pinpoint the true condition of the guest.

Where are you? Are you clothed with Christ? Are you seeking to be reclothed daily to reflect the image in which you were recreated?[11] Or are you trying to dress yourself to be acceptable to your church, community, family, or circle of friends? This is a crucial question because heaven's purpose is to take people who have lost the image of their Creator through sin and reclothe them in Christ to restore them to his image. Nothing short of this transformation is acceptable to the Master of the heavenly wedding banquet.

Admitting that "all our righteous acts are like filthy rags"[12] is a confession that glorifies the righteousness of our perfect God. This confession alone will cause us to resist the temptation to pridefully wear our own religiosity in the presence of God, shunning his righteous Son as our only claim to heaven. When we realize that our undone lives can only be lived in the context of the forgiveness and leadership of God, we will quickly repent and receive his confirmation of our continued place in his circle of love.

> Heaven's purpose is to take people who have lost the image of their Creator through sin and reclothe them in Christ.

The subject of transformation will be discussed throughout this book, but let's nail something down right now: Accepting heaven's message includes Jesus' teaching of the wedding banquet. Coming to the banquet of the kingdom of heaven means having a willingness to be continually changed into the image of God—to be clothed with Christ.

This one fact makes the Bible indispensable to the Christian life. You cannot go to heaven without being clothed with Christ, and you cannot be clothed with Christ apart from his Word. This is not an easy teaching! The message of heaven is living and active. "Sharper than any double-edged sword, it penetrates even to dividing soul and spirit, joints and marrow; it judges the thoughts and attitudes of the heart."[13]

As we conclude this chapter, let me finish the Parable of the Mirror. When we left our weary explorer, he was sitting on top of a mound of rocks, which he had used to cover the offensive mirror. But the mirror under the rocks was as compelling as it was telling. True reflection was better than none at all, and without it, any attempts at improving his life would be futile. The mirror could make all his efforts more efficient and sure. It offered direction on how to restore order, purity, and beauty to his disheveled life. The explorer climbed down off his little mountain of pride, dusted off his bitterness, and began to pull away the stones one at a time until he once again had the mirror in his hands. As he gently hammered out the dents, a reflection of direction began to surface.

With the guidance of his true reflection, the explorer began the process of transformation. He washed off the dirt from his body, he smoothed his hair, he tended his wounds, and he mended his clothing. With renewed vigor, he took up his journey once again, his purpose clearly set before him.

Maybe the value of the mirror to each individual has a lot to do with what we decide to see. Please enter the next few chapters with confidence that God can reveal the reality of your need for him, as well as his own awesome holiness, without scaring you away. In him and his mirror you will find the power to transform your image as heaven works in your real world.

4

Heaven's Call

Wholehearted Obedience

The young lady on the phone was sobbing. Her best friend was in a coma at a local hospital—possibly poisoned. The family wanted to talk to a minister but had no church connection. She asked me to go see them and try to help.

Arriving at the Intensive Care Unit, I identified the mother by the look of silent terror in her eyes. Following brief introductions, mother, step-father, and younger brother stood vigil as I made my way back to her room. Debbie's (not her real name) motionless body was like the eye of a hurricane. A storm of doctors, nurses, tubes, and machines swirled around her bed. Sadly, the doctor's face told the terminal story.

I returned to the family and gathered them in the hospital chapel. We knelt down to pray. *But to whom? And for what?* I knew that it was not commitment to him that motivated their prayer. I led the prayer, but I felt so empty.

We returned to the ICU waiting area. A tormented recounting by her brother of the party where she first fell revealed that she had poisoned herself. No, not suicide. It was completely unintentional. She had gone to a spiritualist and psychic to buy some herbal teas for good luck—"teas with the power to make her life better." Then later at the party, she passed out immediately after drinking the fateful brew.

> Distance from God leaves us vulnerable to a pattern of life that often scars us before it scares us.

Upon gaining consciousness for a brief moment, she whispered to her brother that she had mixed them too strong and had drunk too much. She then lapsed into an irreversible coma and died eight days later. The autopsy showed a massive hemorrhage in her brain.

Praying to God in the shadow of tragedy is the right thing to do. But such "emergency-motivated" cries for help set God up to seem distant, uninterested, and unable to help. Unless crisis spurs a change of heart and mind, God is, in human terms, in a no-win situation. Sudden "faith" in God, spawned in a moment of extreme need, has no root.

I don't mean to sound critical. I'm not saying that we shouldn't pray to God in the midst of our tragedy. What I am saying is that tragedies like Debbie's are played out in millions of lives every day—not necessarily with psychic teas and caskets, but with consequences no less grave. Distance from God leaves us vulnerable to a *pattern of life* that often scars us before it scares us. Many people don't even realize the extent of their scar tissue until they attempt to stretch out into a relationship and are faced with an invisible, yet immovable barrier. They are desensitized to the ferocity of life's potential consequences because their descent into distance is gradual. Instead of choosing to grow close to God through a lifestyle of obedience to his commands, they keep him at a distance until it appears he can do something they want. Not unlike Debbie, some of us are in critical condition long before we end up in critical care. And then, it's often too late.

> Instead of choosing to grow close to God through a lifestyle of obedience to his commands, they keep him at a distance until it appears he can do something they want.

Wholehearted Obedience

If we want to experience the transforming power of heaven in our real world, we must be willing to accept the whole message of heaven. Heaven's message of *newness* centers around a new relationship with God. As we've already seen in the first three chapters, this new relationship with God restores our value, offers forgiveness for our sins, and transforms our images. A fourth aspect of heaven's message of newness is the call to wholehearted *obedience* to God's commands.

But obedience is not a concept that Americans readily take to. Our pride and independence make obedience an unpopular concept. Like the Rich Young Ruler in Matthew 19, we are willing to obey as long as the terms fit our agenda. Let's listen in on the young ruler's conversation with Jesus:

> Now a young man came up to Jesus and asked, "Teacher, what good thing must I do to get eternal life?"
>
> "Why do you ask me about what is good?" Jesus replied. "There is only One who is good. If you want to enter life, obey the commandments."
>
> "Which ones?" the man inquired.
>
> Jesus replied, "Do not murder, do not commit adultery, do not steal, do not give false testimony, honor your father and mother, and love your neighbor as yourself."
>
> "All these I have kept," the young man said. "What do I still lack?"
>
> Jesus answered, "If you want to be perfect, go sell your possessions and give to the poor, and you will have treasure in heaven. Then come, follow me."
>
> When the young man heard this, he went away sad, because he had great wealth.

Then Jesus said to his disciples, "I tell you the truth, it is hard for a rich man to enter the kingdom of heaven. Again I tell you, it is easier for a camel to go through the eye of a needle than for a rich man to enter the kingdom of God."[1]

This man's affections were divided. He had a degree of love for heavenly treasure, but he also loved his earthly treasures. Jesus taught, "store up [for yourselves] treasures in heaven . . . for where your treasure is, there your heart will be also."[2] The reason for this, Jesus explains, is that, "No one can serve two masters."[3] Whoever has your heart will have your obedience. Paul adds that our obedience comes from the heart.[4] Wholehearted obedience is powered by concentrating our affection on Jesus.

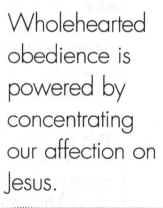

Wholehearted obedience is powered by concentrating our affection on Jesus.

Jesus was not trying to make an impossible request of the rich young ruler just to keep him away. Jesus wanted this man to obey the Law, but even more, Jesus wanted this young man to obey God—wholeheartedly. And as simple as it may sound, obeying God wholeheartedly boils down to following his instructions.

I was fourteen, and the menu was homemade pizza. My mom had purchased all the necessary ingredients in the correct quantities, with a little extra for "recipe mismanagement." The instructions were clear, concise, and complete. What could possibly go wrong?

I started out well—following the instructions on the recipe. Okay . . . let's see . . . "beat eggs in separate bowl until yellow consistency is achieved." Check! Add flour, milk, salt—measure, sift, pinch, pour, stir. Everything was going great, and it seemed so easy. *This is a breeze*, I thought. *I've got a future in television; the next Frugal Gourmet! I must be a natural.*

Who needs a recipe? Grated cheese, pepperoni, olives, sauce. Into the bowl it *all* went. *Hmmm.* (Now don't get too far ahead of me here!) You know, I couldn't help but begin to wonder, *How is that cheese and pepperoni going to make its way to the top, at the proper layer, and all spread out in those pretty geometric designs like the professionals?* Something's amiss!

As I stared through the oven window at the swelling, bubbling, and gurgling mass, I was reminded of the movie, *The Blob.* Instead of a masterpiece, I had a master-mess.

Although I was a rookie at cooking, my mom was not one at parenting. She had already purchased enough ingredients for a second try, anticipating that making dinner might become secondary to learning a lesson about following instructions. And although it came a little late, an edible pizza did finally emerge for general consumption.

Those who try to live life by their own recipe end up with a mess on their hands—like my first pizza. They begin with their spiritual recipe in hand, but quickly lay it aside. One decision at a time, they attempt to mix light and dark— the things of the world with the things of God. Soon, they are embarrassed by what they have cooked up or angered by what life has served up. Their recipe never seems to smell, look, or taste as nice as the feast on someone else's table. What is wrong with the mix?

The problem is an unwillingness to use just the ingredients God calls for. Wholehearted obedience means following *his* recipe instead of attempting to mix his with ours. Even Peter found himself being rebuked by Jesus because he did "not have in mind the things of God, but the things of men."[5] This type of would-be disciple simply does not mature. Their life is so full of everything that they cannot focus on anything. And then they begin to believe that God does not have transforming power, that heaven is not really capable of making a difference in their real world. But the problem is not heaven's lack of potency but their lack of single-minded devotion. James states that the double-minded person will receive nothing from the Lord. Not that God doesn't have plenty to give, but that their plates are too full to receive his blessings, and they are not willing to give up anything to make room.

The message of heaven is one of *relationship with God.* But in order for our relationship with God to be what he wants it to be, we must live our lives by his recipe, in *fruitful* obedience.

The Fruits of Obedience

What fruits are we to have in our lives? What fruits demonstrate that we have answered heaven's call to wholehearted obedience? Let's examine some of these fruits.

The fruit of repentance

Those of us who develop a sit-down-across-from-each-other relationship, like Matthew describes, will begin to exhibit the fruit of *repentance*. When we allow God to move into our lives—as Mark implies—we will change the way we respond to sin and temptation. If we have the heart that Luke refers to, we will guard and protect our new life, and true external changes will be evident.[6]

The fruit of the Spirit

Although love, joy, peace, patience, kindness, goodness, faithfulness, gentleness, and self-control exist in some form among people who are not filled with the Word and Spirit of God, Jesus makes it clear that the level of these qualities in the life of a Christian is infinitely higher.[7] When God dwells in us richly, we will lay our lives down to keep our vows of love and commitment to him.

The fruit of righteousness

Jesus taught of a righteousness that came from the inside out—a righteousness not based on appearances.[8] People in all generations are addicted to appearance over substance. Even many churches make decisions based on attendance and contribution versus internal changes that reflect the call of heaven to obedience. The heart filled with the righteous ways of Jesus will pump righteousness into every action of the body, no matter what the situation.[9]

The fruit of the lips

"Out of the overflow of the heart the mouth speaks"—both good and bad.[10] Jesus taught his disciples that the thermometer of the soul is the tongue. If the tongue offers the "sacrifice of praise—the fruit of lips that confess his name"[11]—then the soul is filled with the Spirit's fire. However, if our tongues are full of careless words, caustic gossip and the cursing of our fellow man, then our souls are set on fire by hell. The tongue is the fruit of seeds sown in the heart. When people regularly spend time with God, the results will be obvious in the fruit of their lips. And according to James, no other test is more telling than what comes out of our mouths. Is your tongue controlled by heaven or taken captive by hell?[12]

Jesus taught his disciples that the thermometer of the soul is the tongue.

The fruit of generosity

Paul described the generosity of the Gentile Christians in feeding the hungry in Jerusalem as "fruit."[13] Those who have come to know Christ and cherish his charity toward them cannot help but desire to bless others. The motto of their soul is, "Freely we have received, freely give." These people search out opportunities to bless others at their own expense. Their satisfaction comes from the joy of imitating Jesus.[14]

The fruit of sharing our faith

The most basic truth of Genesis chapter one is that "kind begets kind." Everyone and everything, including God himself, begets another generation that bears its image. In John 4, Jesus described evangelism by using the Greek word for *bearing fruit*.[15] The word in John 4:36 translated "crop" in the New International Version is the same Greek word translated "fruit" in several passages mentioned above.[16] When we get to know Jesus through time spent with him, allowing him to change us internally and retaining what we have gained through him, we will become powerful witnesses to the world. Like spiritual Johnny Appleseeds, we will plant seeds of the Gospel everywhere we go.

The five fruits discussed above are manifestations of wholehearted obedience, and such obedience is an essential part of our relationship with heaven. We can't just ignore God and his commands when life is going well and then demand that he work "magic" in our lives when things get desperate. Like the family of the young woman who died from an overdose of herbal teas, our prayers will be empty if only prayed in the heat of crisis.

I have met many people who are angry at God because he didn't heal on time, get their child off drugs, keep them out of jail, keep them from getting pregnant, and the list goes on.

Such people don't see obedience as a means of working through their problems. They see God more like a genie to be summoned in times of trouble than a God to be served

and obeyed. This is not even remotely close to a transforming discipleship—this is imitation religion. And sad to say,
based on this imitation religion, many have determined that
God didn't care about them, when in reality they didn't care
about him.

In order to learn wholehearted obedience, you must
first focus your spiritual growth on the cultivation of a pure
and honest heart before God. When Jesus came into your life
to save you, he saw you from two perspectives: He saw your
weakness, your ungodliness, your sin, and your hostility,
and he also saw the beautiful soul you were created to be.[17]
When Jesus explained heaven in the real world through the
Parable of the Sower, he made it clear that the differences in
the four kinds of people who respond to the message of
heaven are differences of the heart.[18]

Let me close this section of the book with a testimony
to heaven's power to bring newness to your life.

Sewall and Roberta Magnani are a senior Christian
couple from Portland, Oregon, who have gone on to their
reward in heaven. I met them when I was thirteen years old.
Sewall looked like a character straight out of a Herman
Melville novel. At seventy-five, he was as strong as ever,
with a full head of wind-swept, glistening, silver hair. His
weathered face and leathered hands only began to tell the
adventure-filled story of forty years of professionally fishing
the U.S. Pacific coast.

He could do anything—build, plant, trim, paint, hoist
giant loads on his powerful shoulders, pet a kitten, rescue a
fallen wren, or gently pat a young boy's shoulder.

His wife of over fifty years, Roberta, was a stick of Christian dynamite. At less than five feet tall, she towered in Christian stature. She ran a thrift store to help the poor and gave all the proceeds to Christian education. She made thousands of crafts for the same purpose. When their son died at sea in a raging Pacific storm, they sold his fishing boat and founded a Christian scholarship fund in his honor.

I moved away from Oregon, and while in college, married Susan. Sewall and Roberta watched over us as their own. Every time we visited Oregon, we would go to their home and bask in their example of straightforward devotion to accepting the message of heaven as their exclusive guide for life.

They see God more like a genie to be summoned in times of trouble rather than a God to be served and obeyed.

Upon returning to college after one such visit, a letter came, signed only by Roberta. Sewall had suffered a massive stroke, and was totally disabled. Unable to even speak his own name, he was completely bedridden. We corresponded over the next twenty months until another break in school provided us the opportunity to visit.

It was hard to see Sewall like that. His precious little wife, still full of enthusiasm and energy, had rechanneled her strength to loving and serving her husband. Bathing so gently, feeding so patiently, caressing so compassionately—he was still her man.

My wife has been blessed with a beautiful singing voice, and Roberta asked Susan to sing some favorite hymns for Sewall at his bedside. Roberta set up a small tape recorder to record Susan singing hymns for Sewall, so that she could play it for him after we left. I sat down by the bed and reached over to hold his hand. It was still his hand—weathered and warm.

Oh, how I wished he could speak. Just his name, my name. Anything. Susan began to sing, and I saw his eyes shift under those silver brows. A twinkle came. She sang,

> When we walk with the Lord
> In the light of his Word,
> What a glory he sheds on our way!
> While we do his good will,
> He abides with us still,
> And with all who will trust and obey.

And then, after eighteen months of silence, came the duet: Susan and Sewall,

> Trust and obey, for there's no other way,
> To be happy in Jesus, but to trust and obey.

Sewall and Susan were singing together! Roberta and I were weeping. Sewall never spoke again. Although his mind couldn't find its way into speech, his heart was so full of his relationship with God for over fifty years, that it didn't need to summon his mind to find an expression of trust and praise. That one hymn carried Roberta through his passage to heaven and her eventual reunion with him.

Sewall and Roberta answered heaven's call to whole-hearted obedience, and they knew God's presence in their world. He was in them and they in him. How does this happen? How do humans know such peace?

Listen to the song of the Sons at Korah:

> Show us your unfailing love, O Lord,
>> and grant us your salvation.
>
> I will listen to what God the Lord will say;
>> he promises peace to his people, his saints—
>> but let them not return to folly. . . .
>
> Love and faithfulness meet together;
>> righteousness and peace kiss each other.
>> *Faithfulness springs from the earth,*
>> *and righteousness looks down from heaven.*[19]

The presence of God and his peace that passes all understanding are promised to you. Like the gentle and reassuring kiss of Roberta on Sewall's cheek, our faithfulness reaches out to God, and his peace and righteousness greet us with a kiss—the *kiss of God.*

> The message is simply this: You are worth more than heaven to Jesus.

What then does God ask of us? Be faithful to him in your heart, in whatever state you are. Be confident that the Lord is your helper. Seek his heart for comfort, his headship for guidance, and his hand for strength.

The result of such a walk with God is the experience of heaven in your real world. The message of heaven must be heard and trusted—heard in a personal way, person to person from God to you. And the message must be lived in trusting faith. The message is simply this: You are worth more than heaven to Jesus, so he offered you total pardon from the guilt and punishment of your sin. He took your sin away and came to live in you, so that through wholehearted obedience you could be transformed back into the image in which you were created.

What other message on earth have you accepted in place of this one? What other message offers what this one brings to your life? What are you waiting for? Begin by accepting the message of heaven. Study it. Keep seeking to understand the message to which God calls you. Invite God to make changes in your life through what you learn in his message. Hang on to it for all your worth. This is the beginning of heaven in your real world.

Imitating Heaven's Model

Model

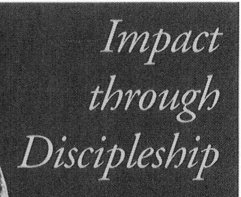

Impact through Discipleship

Part Two Prelude

If a picture is worth a thousand words, how blessed we are that in the grace of God he gave us both the picture (Jesus) and the words (the Bible). Jesus Christ came as a model for believers. He came to show us the life of our heavenly Father in whose image we were created.

> In the beginning was the Word, and the Word was with God, and the Word was God.
>
> The Word became flesh and made his dwelling among us. We have seen his glory, the glory of the One and Only, who came from the Father, full of grace and truth. . . .
>
> No one has ever seen God, but God the One and Only, who is at the Father's side, *has made him known*.[1]

The Greek word translated "has made him known," means to *lead out, explain, report, describe, bring news of.* After observing and comprehending Jesus' example, we are to *imitate* heaven's model.

Jesus carried the entire and complete image of God in his earthly life.

> For in Christ all the fullness of the Deity lives in bodily form, and you have been given fullness in Christ who is the head over every power and authority.[2]

Jesus is the fullness of God incarnate, in the flesh. This is why he could say in John 14:9, "Anyone who has seen me has seen the Father."

Just as Jesus is the fullness of God, we are the fullness of Christ.

> And God placed all things under his feet and appointed him [Christ] to be head over everything for the church, which is his body, the fullness of him who fills everything in every way. [3]

As the fullness of Christ, we are to imitate him.

> Be imitators of God, therefore, as dearly loved children and live a life of love, just as Christ loved us and gave himself up for us as a fragrant offering and sacrifice to God.[4]

> I [Jesus] have set you an example that you should do as I have done for you.[5]

To this you were called, because Christ suffered for you, leaving you an example, that you should follow in his steps.[6]

Jesus left us an example. John calls it a *pattern* or *model* to follow. Peter calls it a *pattern to be copied down,* as a drawing or a writing. Paul tells us to mimic this drawing of the image of heaven in the real world.

In this section of the book, we are going to look at four powerful characteristics of the life heaven calls us to live in this real world. We are going to learn these qualities through the One and Only who came to this earth to make God known to us. The four characteristics are the touch, sight, voice, and heart of heaven. We will study heaven in the real world of Jesus to find a pattern to follow for experiencing heaven in our real world.

Just as Jesus is the fullness of God, we are the fullness of Christ.

Throughout this section, keep two doctrines in mind. First, Jesus is the fullness of heaven on earth during his ministry; so whatever he does or says is exactly what the Father in heaven would do in that situation. Second, we are called to imitate his model so that we can demonstrate heaven in the real world through following him.

5 Imitating Heaven's Touch

Becoming the Hands of Heaven

Proper Jewish women didn't think of letting their hair down in public. But this woman had neither the time nor the pride to consider such nuances of etiquette. Her life was a wreck. Her emotions, a storm. Her sin, a prison. Luke 7 records the story: She must have cringed at the thought of subjecting herself to the scrutiny of the Pharisees. The "Separate Ones," as they called themselves, openly despised women like her, considering her very presence a blight. Her name in a conversation was simply a segue to the evils of sin and the surety of God's wrath.

But when she learned that Jesus was at the home of a nearby Jewish religious leader, her desire to be near him was more powerful than the certain distance she would feel from the others.

As was the customary setting, the meal took place around a relatively low table surrounded by cushions. The guests reclined on one arm, stretching their legs out away from the table. She entered the room and was instantly overcome by emotion. Jesus remained still and calm as she broke into tears at his feet. With a display that would have overwhelmed a stoic, her emotions flooded over his feet in her tears. To Jesus, she was making known her love. To the others, she was making a scene.

> To Jesus, she was making known her love. To the others, she was making a scene.

She was close enough to hear what Jesus could hear. Simon, the host of the banquet, said, "If this man were a prophet, he would know who is touching him and what kind of woman she is—that she is a sinner." The judgment against her was now passing to him. Would Jesus choose acceptance among them over touching her life? Would Jesus bow to the pressure of his host?

Jesus looked at the woman but spoke to Simon. What did she see in his eyes? Did she even hear what he said? His gaze was so captivating. She became the center of Jesus' attention, the star of his show, the physical illustration of his lesson to Simon. No longer was she an outcast. Her position in the circle of Jesus' love was the most secure in the room!

He called her a giver, a lover, a woman of faith; he offered her forgiveness and peace.

Oh, the amazement of the religious establishment! Heaven went around them to work its miracle of nearness in the real world for a woman they wouldn't even recognize as human.

Our society relates well to this woman. People today are desperately pursuing nearness. No pain is greater than undesired isolation. A phenomenal number of children are estranged from their parents. Fifty percent of our married population have been emotionally labeled "unchosen" by their former mates. The dream of children who visit every Christmas and lifelong mates has faded for many. Satan has pushed the "separation of church and state."

When our elderly neighbor, Lois, was in her final hours, our whole family gathered with her son around her hospital bed. Her body was ravaged by cancer and racked with pain. As we quietly visited for the last time, she refused to complain, but in a particularly difficult moment, she mentioned that her ankles were so sore. Before any of the adults could react, our son Aaron, who was six at the time, placed his soft little hands on her right ankle and began to lightly rub them. Every adult in the room was instantly touched by this spontaneous act of the heart, but none more than Lois. A tear of thankfulness flowed from her eye as a tear of deep respect flowed from mine. *Touch.*

What is it like to be touched by heaven? How does the touch of God feel? Touch is at the heart of Jesus' model of heaven on earth. He will not snub, ignore, or refuse to touch anyone—no matter their condition. Heaven knows how important touch is to humans. Notice with me who heaven touches.

Heaven touches those who have isolating physical illnesses. In Mark 1:40–45 we find Jesus touching a man isolated from his family and friends by the infirmity of leprosy. Leprosy is a dreadful disease in which death literally lives in the extremities of the victims. Due to the deadly effects of the disease, the lepers of Jesus' time were required to be walking billboards of their condition. Commanded by the law to stay away from others, they were required to verbally announce their uncleanness to all.

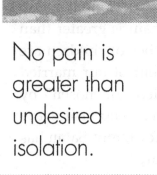

No pain is greater than undesired isolation.

When heaven came to earth, however, lepers were touched. And the healing they experienced was deeper than just a physical cure for the ailments of this life. The touch of heaven restored their value.

I experience the transformation of heaven's touch every time I hug an AIDS patient. I sense it in the grip of weary hands in the circle of prayer in a hospital room. I feel it in the joyful embrace at the finish line of the special olympics. The touch of heaven brings healing to the soul.

Heaven touches those who are in distress. When Jesus' disciples cried out in fear at his transfiguration, he touched them and said, "Don't be afraid."[1] What does a reassuring hand on your shoulder mean when your own hands are resting on the casket of one whose death has left you broken and afraid? Is there any feeling like the touch of your

Father's hand when the darkness of night is as thick as molasses?

Heaven touches the untouchables. Over and over in the Gospels, Jesus is confronted by demon-possessed people. These people had a spiritual problem that caused them to be treated like a social plague. In Mark 3:10 we find Jesus more than willing to touch, and be touched, by them.

I will never be more impacted spiritually than by a brother in Christ named Jim who took me with him to visit a nursing home in Ohio. The young man Jim went to visit was a quadriplegic. He was no relation to Jim at all, except that Jim saw in him a person who longed to be loved.

This man, whose mental capacity was severely limited by the same disease that imprisoned him in a wheelchair, probably evoked the same reaction today as did the people of Jesus' day who were demon possessed. I am not comparing mental illness to demon possession. I am saying that the two conditions leave their victims on the list of the socially unacceptable, the untouchables. But both Jesus and his followers refuse to accept this societal excommunication.

Jim greeted the man with a hug, and then began to feed him his dinner. During the entire meal, the man flailed his head about, drooling saliva down his face and onto Jim's hands and wrists. Every once in a while, the dripping saliva was slung onto Jim's face by the uncontrolled jerking of the young man's head.

Never did Jim flinch or complain. In fact, he smiled all the way through the visit and all the way home. He never once spoke of the encounter as sacrifice or labor. He really did want to touch one whose mental, emotional, and

spiritual condition made any attempt at mainstream relationships impossible. Jesus touched the untouchables with
the righteous hope of God.

Heaven touches children. Even to the disciples, children
were not considered important or valuable. But heaven has
a different feeling about those whom society would consider
a liability. Jesus made it clear that children are important by
touching them and hugging them to his chest. Notice what
Jesus did to demonstrate the value of children in Mark
10:13–14: "People were bringing little children to Jesus to
have him touch them, but the disciples rebuked them. When
Jesus saw this, he was indignant. He said to them, 'Let the
little children come to me, and do not hinder them, for the
Kingdom of God belongs to such as these.' "

Heaven touches the unclean. In Luke's account of Jesus'
life,[2] he records Jesus coming upon a funeral procession for
a young man. The mother, a widow at that, was so overcome
with grief that a large crowd had come to comfort her. Jesus
could have let the funeral procession pass. He even could
have done the miracle from afar so as to not risk the penalty
of religious separation that followed touching unclean
things—and a dead man was most definitely unclean!

However, Jesus did not focus on his own life and
needs. He saw a widow, who was overcome with hurt, and
he decided to help her. Even if Jesus had not raised the child
from the dead, his simple proximity to the dead man's cof-
fin spoke volumes about Jesus' willingness to touch even
the unclean. The heart of heaven moved the hands of
heaven.

Those who need new life spiritually are desperate for the touch of heaven, and *we* can bring it to their lives. Many people have intricate facades they adeptly use to give off the appearance of life, when in reality, most of them are not far from death. They may not be physically dead—like the young man Jesus raised—but many have a sense that life has passed them by or a feeling that they "might as well be dead." Heaven touches such people, and so must we. And in order to be heaven's hands, we must desire heaven's heart; the compassion of heaven needs to fill us as it did Jesus.

We need a revival among us—a revival of compassion that touches the world with the loving hands of heaven. To help get the revival going, I'll share a few practical examples of how to spread the touch of heaven in your community.

The first example comes from the third- and fourth-grade Sunday school class in our church family. I had preached that God calls us in the Great Commission of Matthew 28:19 to teach disciples of Jesus to obey him. This is different than merely teaching them his commands. It is much more difficult to teach someone to *obey* the command than it is to teach them to *know* the command. Yet, commands have no transforming power without obedience.

> Churches that focus on teaching commands, and not on teaching disciples to obey the commands, are not following what Jesus said.

Churches that focus on teaching commands, and not on teaching disciples to obey the commands, are not following what Jesus said and are denying their members the power that comes from obedience.

My wife and another Christian woman, both of whom are addicted to Jesus and living his commands, made a plan to teach the third and fourth graders how to touch others with love as Jesus did.

They brought all the children from the Sunday school class to our home on a Sunday afternoon. Step one of the plan was to teach the children how to bake a pie. How? By actually taking the children through our kitchen in groups of three and having them make the pies with their own hands.

Step two, while the pies were in the oven, was to teach the children what the Bible says about caring for others the way heaven cares. They learned about Jesus taking time to touch the sick and lonely. Then they practiced ministry. They played the roles of older people who were sick or lonely. They learned how to go into their homes with respect. They walked through how they would give the pie, give their hugs, listen carefully, sing their song, and leave the home with a blessing.

Step three was to load onto the church van and travel to three homes of people in our church. The first stop was at the home of a couple who simply needed encouragement. Next, they visited a new Christian from our senior citizens ministry who was in her final stages of a terminal bout with cancer. The third visit was with an elderly sweetheart who made the children feel as if they had changed her entire world by their visit.

Teaching such young hands to let heaven touch others through them will forever mold how they view themselves and others. We need more Sunday schools that understand the difference between studying the example of heaven's touch and actually touching someone on behalf of heaven.

The second example came one Sunday morning. Halfway through our worship assembly, we always stop and welcome each other. I call it "howdy doody" time. Normally, I can only greet people close to the front because the aisle quickly fills with huggers and handshakers, but on this particular morning, the center aisle was strangely empty. I looked toward the back of the auditorium and immediately understood why. I noticed a visitor in the rear of the auditorium, right in the center aisle. He was very tall, had long hair, and was dressed completely in black leather. His most noticeable "adornment" was an earring in his left ear. It had feathers hanging from it, reaching clear down to the pocket of his leather vest.

I imagined for a moment that Moses had entered our assembly, for as he started to walk up the aisle, he parted our assembly right down the middle. I felt frustrated and headed toward him. But before I could get to him with my *Why am I the only guy who's gonna touch him* attitude, Sim came to the rescue. Sim is a ninety-year-old Christian who understands the touch of heaven. (He also has a hug that feels like a Heimlich maneuver!) He came right out of his pew, introduced himself to the "renegade," hugged him, and insisted he sit with him and his wife, Marie.

I thought to myself, *That is exactly what Jesus would have done!* That is the touch of heaven.

Christians like you and me must take a fresh look at how the life of Jesus reveals the touch of heaven and then imitate that model. Our world is desperate for heaven's life-giving touch. Satan has come to touch the world, but he kills, steals, and destroys. We are more often like Pilate than Jesus; we simply wash our hands of the world's troubles. We retreat to our sanctuaries of ceremony where we teach the touch of heaven, but we do not touch. How can we claim to be his body if we disconnect ourselves when the head calls us to be his hands? Reach out and touch someone with the touch of heaven.

We retreat to our sanctuaries of ceremony where we teach the touch of heaven, but we do not touch.

6

Imitating Heaven's Look

....

Reflecting the Eyes of Heaven

"Just one look. That's all it took, baby, just one look." I would like to see a book cataloging looks and what they mean. A look can say it all.

- My dad had that under-the-eyebrows, over-the-newspaper, "You'd better think before you act" look.

- I was exposed to the famous "You can't be serious" look from girls I asked out in high school.

- Police officers taught me the slowly-remove-the-mirrored-shades, cock-your-head-to-one-side, "You're in a heap of trouble" look.

- My mom was a pro at the "Give it your best expla-anation for being late" look.

What look would *heaven* give you? Speaker and author Jeff Walling described the looks many Christians suppose they would receive from God.

One was the *snub*. This look basically communicated that, although you would be allowed into heaven, you certainly were not God's little pride and joy. A second expected look was this: "Well, well, well. Everybody look who we have here! Come forward and let everybody get a real good look at an example of what *not* to be." A third look was from the black-robed judge coming over the judge's bench with a "You're going straight to hell" look in his eyes. But Jeff then asked an appropriate question: "Where did we get the idea that these are the looks we can anticipate from God?" We certainly didn't get these ideas from God!

What do you see when you look into the eyes of heaven? And since we are the body of Christ imitating the model of heaven, what reflection do others see when they look into our eyes?

What did Jesus' presence on earth teach us about the eyes of heaven? Jesus told the Jews in John 5:37 that they had "never seen [God's] form." Although this infuriated them, Jesus knew he had to expose their picture of God as incomplete and incorrect. Through the teaching and example of Jesus, we can see what heaven sees and thus reflect the eyes of God to the world.

Heaven sees us personally. This truth is born out over and over in Scripture but nowhere more poignantly than Luke 8:40–48. Jesus is swarmed by the multitude, and the disciples are swept away in the triumphant procession. In the crowd was a woman who saw the touch of heaven as her only hope. The doctors had her money, but she had no cure. She needed to touch Jesus.

When she touched him, Jesus immediately responded. He had to know who it was that had that kind of faith, that level of hope and determination. She was afraid, and the disciples were indignant. How could anyone be concerned about an individual when you have the crowd to keep you busy? But heaven was.

One phrase in this passage will forever change you: "Then the woman, *seeing that she could not go unnoticed. . . .*"[1] Heaven had *noticed* her. She could not hide from the eyes of heaven. God was going to heal more than her body. Jesus literally pulled this woman to the surface of that sea of humanity. He would not allow her to sink back to the bottom and stay in oblivion.

Heaven also saw the personal value of the sinful woman in Luke 7. The religious establishment viewed people like her as good for nothing but condemning conversations. Jesus made her a star example of love and faith. Jesus' indicting question to Simon underscored the difference between the eyes of "religious" people and the eyes of heaven.

"Then [Jesus] turned toward the woman and said to Simon, 'Do you *see* this woman?' " The answer communicated by Simon's thoughts in verse 39 is a terse "no!" Simon didn't even see a person. He saw nothing but a dreadful disease tarnishing his image.

When we imitate the model of heaven in how we view others, we see kings in shepherd boys, prophets in farmers, and preachers in persecutors.

And how about the affect of heaven's love on Zacchaeus? Jesus looked up and said with his eyes, "You matter. You have value."

What do your eyes say? When people come under the watchful eye of your church, do they feel comforted or condemned? Shepherded or herded? Do you make them feel like they're a name on your heart or a number in the pew?

When we imitate the model of heaven in how we view others, we unleash the power of personal vision. We see kings in shepherd boys, prophets in farmers, supporters of the ministry in the demon-possessed, and preachers in persecutors.

When we look at others the way Jesus does, we are more careful and respectful. Everyone counts. When the world is ogling the ninety-nine, God's people are taking risks for the one.[2] When people who are led by their religion look down on others,[3] those led by the example of Christ cherish the value of all.[4]

The eyes are a window to the soul. A simple look will reveal the tenant of your soul. Do others see Christ or Satan reflected when they look into your eyes?

Heaven sees us internally. Jesus said, "You are the ones who justify yourselves in the eyes of men, but God knows your hearts. What is highly valued among men is detestable in God's sight."[5] This truth is a double-edged sword, depending on the condition of our hearts. If we are strutting around in our religious circles seeking influence and positions of honor among people, God is not impressed. In fact, all such pride is a declaration of war against him. On the other hand, when others take offense at you and withhold their love and support from you, God still knows you and sees your internal devotion to him.

Jesus also taught that God sees our anonymous service done for others,[6] and he is pleased with the invisible, internal motives of our hearts. This teaching flies directly in the face of the world's main motivation for serving. God will reward you beyond your wildest dreams for your unseen acts of kindness.

Many among us are addicted to appearance, and it comes out in how we see. Some people put much stock in how those who lead the worship assembly are dressed. But such external emphasis is a satanic diversion from the true calling of being clothed with Christ. Some Christians are more devoted to mimicking fashion models than to imitating heaven's model. Their souls are in rags while their bodies are draped with the world's fashion. Their bodies are in vogue while their souls are void of compassion, kindness, humility, gentleness, and patience.[7]

Jesus is not the tailor of our Sunday-go-to-meeting mentality. We must repent of our worldliness. I have met people throughout my two decades in the church who do nothing for the cause of Christ, yet they are dressed great for "going to church." I'm not against women wearing dresses and men wearing ties, but I am at war with the priority of the external over the internal. Some of the same people who will pay a hundred dollars to array their grandchild for Easter Sunday will turn right around and resist the clothing Christ seeks to put on them.

Jesus shredded the external facade of the Pharisees on nearly every available occasion. He was so disgusted with their infantile attraction to tassels, titles, and tithes that he dubbed them hypocrites, blind fools, whitewashed tombs, and snakes! And all too often, the Pharisees' shoes fit us as well. Much of the light within us is darkness;[8] and we need the light of heaven to shine on us anew.

> Some Christians are more devoted to mimicking fashion models than to imitating heaven's model.

Heaven sees us eternally. Ultimately, it is the eternal lens that brings everything else into focus. "So we fix our eyes not on what is seen, but on what is unseen. For what is seen is temporary, but what is unseen is eternal."[9] Jesus explained his demonstration of this truth following the conversion of Zacchaeus. "For the Son of Man came to seek and to save what was lost."[10] Why did Jesus look up at Zacchaeus while others passed him by? Jesus saw him as an eternal soul that needed salvation.

Jesus taught this same lesson to the disciples when he reached out to the Samaritan woman.[11] He drew them into his vision of the world when he commanded, "Open your eyes and look at the fields! They are ripe for harvest."[12] The eternal perspective separates imitation religion from imitators of heaven's model.

The religious leaders wouldn't consider ministering to the sinners of their day because they were too caught up in their religion. They were so concerned with the appearance of their religious organization in the eyes of the world that they didn't have the interest or energy to really seek the praise that comes from God.[13] What was worse, they believed God was like them! They were confident that God would imitate their decisions and actions were he in their position.

To correct their false assumptions about how God views his children, Jesus told the story of the Lost Son.[14] Contrary to their theology, Jesus presented God as a compassionate father overwhelmed with his desire to restore his son to full fellowship. Jesus brought the father's compassion into sharper focus by previewing the feelings of the younger son while he was still away. The boy outlined a four-part speech for his father: (1) I have sinned against heaven. (2) I have sinned against you. (3) I am no longer worthy to be called your son. (4) I am worthy only to be one of your hired servants. The boy felt that he was so separated from the heart of his father that his father would find no worth in him, or at least not enough to be considered a member of the family.

This is precisely what many people in our present society feel toward God. But in Jesus' description of the compassionate heavenly father, the father positioned himself so that as soon as the boy turned toward home, he would sense the loving eyes of his father: "So he got up and went to his father. But while he was a long way off, *his father saw him* and was filled with compassion for him; he ran to his son, threw his arms around him and kissed him."[15]

The father's longing *look* was enough to keep the boy coming closer. The message of the eyes of the father was an unconditional and passionate, "I want you back in our family where you belong."

Had the older brother been the first to spot his wayward and wasteful sibling, the look would have been enough to turn him back to the pigs. The older brother did not share the father's eternal view of the returning son. From the older brother's worldly perspective, his brother was a *loser*. In the father's heavenly eyes, the son was *lost*. We are desperate for more Christians and churches who will repent of looking at the lost as losers.

Jesus uses this description of heaven's view of people to get through to us. God will not allow our cold stares to

> From the older brother's perspective, his brother was a *loser*. In the father's heavenly eyes, the son was *lost*.

stifle his celebration over a restored sinner. Heaven sees people *personally,* *internally,* and *eternally.* Nothing in this world can cloud heaven's perfect view of man's worth and eternal destiny.

Christian songwriters Geoff Moore and Steven Curtis Chapman express it best in a song titled "If You Could See What I See." Although the song specifically addresses the love between a man and a woman, the chorus and second verse genuinely reflect the way God sees you and me.

> *Chorus:*
> And you would know that you have my heart,
> if you could see what I see.
> That a treasure's what you are,
> if you could see what I see.
>
> *Verse 2:*
> I know there are days when you feel,
> so much less than ideal,
> wondering what I see in you.
> It's all of the light and the grace,
> your belief in me drives me to say,
> that "I promise you a faithful love forever true."[16]

As we imitate the model of heaven, our prayer should be that God would grow that kind of love in our hearts for the people around us. Then they would see in our eyes a reflection of the love heaven has for them. The missing punch in many churches and individual Christians will be restored when we model our view of others after the eyes of heaven.

Many people will be impacted for Christ when we imitate his model of looking at others with a view toward reconciliation to God and restoration to his family, the church.

7

Imitating Heaven's Voice

Sharing the Word of Heaven

"Ninety percent of conflict is tone of voice." Communication is a mixture of many components that can carry more than one message at a time. Body language and facial expression often say more than the words that accompany them. I overheard one exasperated mother sternly warn her child, "Don't use that tone of *face* with me, Young Man!" Tone of face?

If you have accepted the message of heaven as true, then you know that what we say reveals our hearts. Jesus and James both give extensive instructions concerning this.[1]

The psalmist David spoke about the connection between heart and mouth. "Though you probe my heart and examine me at night, though you test me, you will find nothing; I have resolved that my mouth will not sin."[2] And again, "May the words of my mouth and the meditation of my heart be pleasing in your sight, O Lord, my Rock and my Redeemer."[3] Solomon continued this theme with, "A wise man's heart guides his mouth, and his lips promote instruction."[4]

Jesus is the model of heaven for his disciples on earth—especially in how we are to use our speech to make an impact for heaven in our real world. Jesus' landmark statement on this topic is recorded in John 12:49–50: "For I did not speak of my own accord, but the Father commanded me *what to say* and *how to say it.* I know that his command leads to eternal life. So whatever I say is just what the Father has told me to say."

Now that is a challenging statement. If any act of obedience and discipleship is difficult and defining, imitating the model of Jesus in our communication has to be at the top of any list.

If dividing and conquering has any place here, then we will look at imitating the model of Jesus' communication from two perspectives: *what to say*, and *how to say it.*

What to Say

We know from section one of this book that heaven's message encourages people to accept God's desire for a relationship with him. This relationship offers value, pardon, transformation, and a call to obedience.

There are many well-known sayings of Jesus, but I'm going to step out on a limb and say that many church-going people learned those phrases as book, chapter, and verse of a particular doctrine, instead of hearing them as the voice of the now-living God.

I want to share with you some of his most impacting statements, realizing that as we follow his model for what to say and how to say it, we will immediately have the opportunity to increase the impact we are making on our world.

In the research for this book, I read through the four Gospels more than thirty times, over the course of eighteen months. At first I saw what I was *taught* to see. Then I saw what I *wanted* to see. Finally I saw what I *needed* to see.

Here is a list of things we need to hear from heaven and then pass on to others as we model our speech after Jesus. (Note: The passages listed are taken primarily from Matthew, Luke, and John due to the immense overlap of Mark in the other Gospels.) Don't read over these words quickly—they are heaven's voice.

- I am willing.[5]

- I will go and heal him.[6]

- Take heart, your sins are forgiven.[7]

- Go learn what this means: "I desire mercy, not sacrifice."[8]

- Come to me, all you who are weary and burdened, and I will give you rest.[9]

- Take courage! It is I. Don't be afraid.[10]

- The Son of Man came not to be served, but to serve.[11]

- What do you want me to do for you?[12]

- Why are you bothering this woman? She has done a beautiful thing to me.[13]

- My Father, if it is not possible for this cup to be taken away unless I drink it, may your will be done.[14]

- Are not five sparrows sold for two pennies? Yet not one of them is forgotten by God. Indeed, the very hairs of your head are all numbered.[15]

- But we had to celebrate and be glad, because this brother of yours was dead and is alive again; he was lost and is found.[16]

- I have prayed for you . . . that your faith may not fail.[17]

- Father, forgive them, for they do not know what they are doing.[18]

- Then neither do I condemn you, go now and leave your life of sin.[19]

- I no longer call you servants. . . . Instead I have called you friends.[20]

- Mary.[21]

- Peace be with you.[22]

- Come and have breakfast.[23]

Every one of these statements is from heaven. Jesus said he didn't say anything that the Father did not give him to say. But I anticipate that at first glance you might question some of my choices.

Okay. Fair enough. But read through the list several times. Think how your family would change if such constant reminders of willingness, forgiveness, rest, and service were spoken in your home. How would your job change if anyone consistently asked, "What do you want me to do for you?" How would your children's Sunday school classes be different if the motto of every adult member of your church was, "I did not come to be served, but to serve." (If you are the education director, you would probably pass out!)

> Think how your family would change if constant reminders of willingness, forgiveness, rest, and service were spoken in your home.

What would the visitors to our church assemblies think if we encouraged everyone with the words of heaven, "Don't bother this woman, she has done a beautiful thing for me," or "We must celebrate." Would they see more tolerance in our posture toward each other's individual expressions of worship? Would they hear a genuine thankfulness in our words toward each other, knowing that Jesus does not condemn us?

Think how much it means to you to hear someone call you "friend" and really treat you as one. Notice how people respond when you tell them, "I have prayed for you."

How does it make us feel just to hear our name—like "Mary"? Just to be reminded that someone knows us well enough to number the hairs on our head. How does it affect your self-esteem when someone invites you to breakfast just to offer you encouragement, rest, and healing?

The tongue modeled after the example of Jesus can be more powerful in healing than a thousand hospitals, more effective in establishing peace than a thousand treaties, more restful to the soul than ten thousand vacations, more impacting to the world than an earthquake.

> The tongue modeled after the example of Jesus can be more powerful in healing than a thousand hospitals.

Heaven is calling you to open your mouth and let the mind of Christ and the heart of God flow through you like a mighty river of living water. I believe if you have read this far, you probably want to fulfill this wonderful ministry of imitating the voice of heaven. I also anticipate your fear of failure when you try. Maybe you have struggled with gossip. You might be privately labeled by others as an inquiring mind with a wagging tongue.

Where do you begin?

How to Say It

Remember that Jesus declared that heaven gave him what to say, *and* how to say it. Jesus is revealing that God the Father controlled not only his message but also his motives. Let's look at how we gain control of the tongue and *learn how to say* the message of heaven.

Confess that the tongue is out of control.

The first step in controlling your tongue is admitting that it is out of control. If you believe you have control of your tongue, you are in trouble and do not know it. The Bible clearly says, "No man can tame the tongue. It is a restless evil full of deadly poison."[24] Only God has the power to control our tongues. You and I need the Holy Spirit's power to keep our mouths from leading us into sin. Galatians 5:22 declares that self-control is a fruit of the Spirit. With the help of God we *can* see improvement in our speech.

My wife and I are both the third children in a trio of siblings. There are many blessings in being the youngest child, but they hardly seem to balance the "been there, done that" response we grew up under in the shadow of older brothers and sisters. As a parent, I am very sensitive to this interaction.

One perfect day in late spring, I was quenching the thirst of my young begonias. My children were enjoying nature's wake from her winter nap, riding their bicycles in the driveway. Amy, our youngest, was three years old. She was riding the training-wheel bike, on which all our children learned to ride, around the driveway circuit.

She rode by with one hand raised high in the air, waving like a Rose Parade float queen. "Look, Dad," she said, "I can ride with one hand!"

> The first step in controlling your tongue is admitting that it is out of control.

Her five-year-old brother, Caleb, was right behind her. In the experienced older sibling intonation he quickly added, "That's nothing, because you still have trai . . ." (As the concerned father and champion of the EYCM—Equality for Youngest Child Movement—I was ready to defend against this blatant older sibling attack.) But Caleb, on his own, stopped in mid-syllable.

He quickly continued with an altered verbal course, "I mean, that's great, Amy!" He then rode close to me, flashed a sly smile, and whispered, "I thought before I spoke."

I ran up behind him and swooped him off his bike, hugged him, and thought, *What a world this could be if only we could all. . . .*

And then something hit me. If I had spoken too soon and disciplined him for what I thought was going to happen, I would have never given Caleb the opportunity to show what was really *in his heart.*

In a concrete way, Caleb showed me how simple the transition from criticism to encouragement can be. Wasn't it Jesus who called us to become like little children so that we could enter the kingdom of heaven?

React to sinful speech as we would react to Satan himself.

A serious change came about in my life concerning my speech through a Greek word study. I was trying to understand the Bible description of gossip and slander so that I could isolate this sin in my life. I wanted to get a description so I could recognize the temptation and fight against it more effectively.

Through this study I made a discovery that still gives me cold chills. The Greek word used for "slander" in Titus 2:3 is *diabolos*. This word is used for Satan himself in both the Old and New Testaments. Friend, gossip and slander are satanic speech. When we gossip or slander, we are like spiritual sewage pipes spewing the toxic messages of hell into the lives of others. The warnings in the Scriptures concerning this are strong.[25]

We must resist the temptation to confess other people's sins. We need to ask ourselves where the script for our conversations is coming from—heaven or hell. We need to search the Gospels thoroughly to see if Jesus would be leading the kind of conversations we are.

Stop using obscene and coarse language.

Nor should there be obscenity, foolish talk, or coarse joking, which are out of place, but rather thanksgiving. . . . Let no one deceive you with empty words, for because of such things God's wrath comes on those who are disobedient. Therefore do not be partners with them."[26]

Many excuses are given by people of all ages for their coarse language: Culture, raising, differences in verbal tolerance, etc., etc. I've used them all and heard them all. But they are simply ungodly excuses for people who are looking for reasons to hang on to a way of life that they did not learn from Jesus.

When we gossip or slander, we are like spiritual sewage pipes spewing the toxic messages of hell into the lives of others.

It took total humiliation to break this stronghold of Satan in my life. I had only been a Christian about three months when I preached what became known as the "swearing sermon." It was my second sermon. I got really wound up and intended to say, "Shoot!" You guessed it. The Lord decided he was going to break me of my lingering profanity. Clear as a bell I said *another* word that begins with *sh*.

The verbal hand grenade exploded all over everybody. After what seemed like, oh—*a year*—the responses began. My wife bowed her head in prayer. Every ounce of blood in my body drained to my feet. I was hot and very dizzy! Roy snickered, Byron shook his head, and Theodore adjusted his hearing aid. Eddie, the only teenager in our church of thirty members, collapsed on the back pew, doubled over with laughter.

Ruby Taylor saved my ministry. This older sister in the faith, sitting right on the front row, hollered, "Just keep on preachin', Honey!" I couldn't that day, but my lesson was learned. God wants speech that reflects heaven.

Exchange satanic speech for the seasoning of heaven.

Changes are made successful by *exchanges*. Paul told the Colossian disciples, "Let your conversation be *always* full of grace, seasoned with salt, so that you may know how to answer everyone."[27] The Ephesian Christians received a similar challenge: "Do not let any unwholesome talk come out of your mouths, but only what is helpful for building others up according to their needs, that it may benefit those who listen."[28]

Within these two verses are crucial motivations for imitating the voice of heaven. First, how we speak greatly affects our opportunities for sharing our faith authentically with unbelievers. Second, it is our responsibility to do what meets other people's needs, benefiting them. Many times I have fallen to verbal sin when my only concern was my *need* to get something off my chest. I rarely considered that they didn't *need* to hear what I was saying, and it certainly didn't *benefit* either one of us!

I am aware that this chapter has not stressed the importance of sharing the true doctrines of the Scriptures. I do believe that it's critical to do so, and therefore I devoted the first section of the book to that emphasis. One of the most dangerous and devastating trends among some Bible believing people is the manner in which they express Bible doctrines. Although we are commanded to "speak the truth in love,"[29] I have personally seen people defend what they believe to be the truth with looks of meanness in their eyes and the sting of hell in their tones. Contending for the faith in a contentious way is an abomination. Using intimidation, exaggeration, and accusation to "promote sound doctrine" is detestable in the eyes of God. Jesus himself said,

> Woe to you teachers of the law and Pharisees, you hypocrites! You shut the kingdom of heaven in men's faces. You yourselves do not enter, nor will you let those enter who are trying to. . . .
>
> You travel over land and sea to win a single convert, and when he becomes one, you make him twice as much a son of hell as you are. . . .
>
> Woe to you, teachers of the law and Pharisees, you hypocrites! You give a tenth of your spices—mint, dill and cumin. But you have neglected the more important matters of the law—justice, mercy and faithfulness. You should have practiced the latter, without neglecting the former. You blind guides! You strain out a gnat but swallow a camel.[30]

For many of us, that lump in our throats is no frog. It isn't even Adam's apple. It is one big, hairy, stinky camel of pride and arrogance. That camel does not know how to say the truth, because we have taken the truth of heaven and shared it with the voice of hell! It is time for repentance in Bible-believing churches. We must turn from our positions of pride in thinking we have the truth, and we must imitate the model of heaven in living the purpose of the truth. God gave the message so that people without hope could find love, pardon, new life, and a purpose to live for.

The world needs to hear a word from heaven, but they need to hear it the way heaven would say it.

As a young married man I used to tell Susan, "Your dress makes you look pretty." It was an okay compliment, and she knew my intentions were pure and true, but one day I heard one of the leaders in our church compliment his wife of fifty years by saying, "You sure make that dress look pretty."

Does what you say matter? Now tell me, does how you say it make a difference?

Those who truly wish to be disciples of heaven's model in the real world will demonstrate their desire by imitating what the voice of heaven says *and* how the voice of heaven says it.

Imitating Heaven's Heart

Demonstrating the Heart of Heaven

Set your hearts on things above, where Christ is seated at the right hand of God.[1]

The heart of Christianity is having the heart of Christ. Nothing can substitute. If Christ doesn't live in your heart, you are simply masquerading as a child of the light. And even though you may feel very confident in your religion, it becomes increasingly obvious by your touch, eyes, and voice that you only experience Christ on the surface.

Two children, Lewis and Herbie, each approached God in prayer. Their prayers are included in the book, *Children's Letters to God.*[2]

Lewis prayed,

> Dear God,
>> Do you remember me? I prayed to you before. I kept my end of the bargain, but you didn't send the horse! What gives?
>>> Signed,
>>> Lewis

Herbie's prayer was very different.

> Dear God,
>> Count me in.
>>> Your friend,
>>> Herbie

Lewis' prayer is where most people's hearts are when they first approach God. In essence, they say, "God, I have a life, and I want you to be in it. I want you to bless my plans and my goals. I want a certain lifestyle, house, relationship, car, job, paycheck, bank account, church, community, level of health, etc., and I expect you to provide it."

Herbie on the other hand is saying, "God, *you have a life, and I want to be in it!* Whatever you are doing in the world today, I want to be right in the middle of your will and work." This is the kind of heart heaven desires.

Christ himself said that, although no doctrine is to be neglected, not all doctrines are of equal importance.[3] In our quest to imitate Christ, we must not bypass imitating his order of priorities. Whatever is the *main thing* to him must become the *main thing* to us.

In Matthew 23:23 Jesus teaches that justice, mercy, and faithfulness are more important matters of the law than the tithe. In a companion passage, Luke adds, "You neglect . . . the love of God."[4] Jesus is not teaching that any commandment is invalid, he is simply getting across the point that heaven has priorities when it comes to obeying principles.

The greatest commandment is love. And the ultimate priority of heaven is love. Take a moment to read the following passages.

> So in everything, do unto others what you would have them do to you, for *this sums up the Law and the prophets.*[5]

> "Love the Lord your God with all your heart and with all your soul and with all your mind." This is the first and greatest commandment. And the second is like it: "Love your neighbor as yourself." *All the Law and the Prophets hang on these two commandments.*[6]

Whatever you are doing in the name of the Lord is without merit or meaning unless you are doing it out of love for God and your fellow disciples.

"Love the Lord your God with all your heart and with all your soul and with all your mind and with all your strength." The second is this: "Love your neighbor as yourself." *There is no commandment greater than these.*[7]

And whatever other commandment there may be are summed up in this one rule: "Love your neighbor as yourself." Love does no harm to its neighbor, therefore, love is the fulfillment of the law.[8]

The entire law is *summed up in a single command,* "Love your neighbor as yourself."[9]

It is abundantly clear that whatever you are doing in the name of the Lord is without merit or meaning unless you are doing it out of love for God and your fellow disciples. I honestly believe there are practicing atheists attending our churches. They live as though having perfect doctrine is the main thing. They teach as though getting people to agree with their interpretation of Scripture is the main thing. And I have been around long enough to see that they may *never* get around to really loving God or anybody else. And they do not teach their followers to love God.

> They teach their listeners that the Bible *says* to love God, but they do not teach their disciples to *love* God.

Now let me get lucid: They teach their listeners that the Bible says to love God, but they do not teach their disciples to love God. The difference is heaven and hell. To them, book, chapter, and verse is treated with higher priority than knowing God. They are practicing atheists because they have more love and devotion to knowing the *Bible* than to knowing the *author* of the Bible.

In many situations, the *main* thing becomes the *missed* thing. In March of 1990, my friend Bill and I fulfilled a life-long dream of going to Egypt. As we approached the Great Pyramids on the golden sands of ancient Giza, awe filled us. There we stood in the footsteps of Moses, Joseph, and Jesus' family. Majestic beyond belief, the lone champions of the Seven Wonders of the Ancient World towered above us. We clamored out of the taxi and ran to take our place in line.

There was just too much to take in for me to concentrate on any one thing. My friend, however, is pragmatism personified. Quickly scanning the terrain, he discovered that there were two lines. As he was calculating which line was the shortest and moving the fastest, he discovered two separate destinations. One line, the one we were *not* in, was moving steadily into the robber's entrance of the Great Pyramid of Cheops. The one we *were* in, by my impulsiveness, was longer, slower, and ended with a five-dollar fee to sit on a sickly, stinky, spitting camel!

We sheepishly stepped from one line to the next. I noted in my mental journal how silly it seemed to travel seven thousand miles and six time zones to the sight of the greatest human accomplishment of the ancient world, only to wait in line and pay to sit on a camel. The *main* thing almost became the *missed* thing. And although we made a successful midcourse correction, we too, for a moment, were in the line awaiting a destiny of minimal return. (To say the least!)

I had not been a Christian for very long when I went as a counselor to a Christian youth retreat in eastern Texas. The director of the weekend retreat asked me if I would "preside at the Lord's Table" during the Sunday morning worship. I nervously agreed to give it my best shot.

There is a very specific order associated with partaking of the unleavened bread and the fruit of the vine in the fellowship of the Bible-believing churches I am associated with. Much of the order is based in biblical example, while some has no sacred origin. The key doctrines of the Lord's Supper are remembering the Lord's sacrifice, recognizing the body of the Lord, examining our relationship with Christ and his body, and proclaiming the Lord's death until he comes.

When my turn came to get up and draw the group's attention to the Lord's supper, my nervousness got the best of me. I got a little confused and didn't get the order quite right. I simply said one prayer for both the unleavened bread, which represents the body of Christ, and the wine, which represents the blood of Christ. Then I took both trays at the same time and gave them to the first row of worshipers.

I knew I was in trouble from the very first guy. He took the bread, broke a piece off and ate it. But when I handed him the tray of individual glasses of wine, he wasn't sure what to do.

Confused? Let me explain. You see, in our tradition, we have an order for the Lord's Supper: pray—pass (the

> Every command ever given bows in submission to the greatest of all commands —to love God and each other.

bread)—pause—pray—pass (the wine). I accidentally blew the whole service with my out-of-order pray—pass—pass.

Because I failed to pray—pass—pause—pray—pass, each person, one at a time, took a small glass of wine, said their own individual prayer to make up for my mistake, and then took the bread.

Some may be thinking, "Good. At least someone had the presence of mind to get things straightened out!" Others might be thinking, "What in the world are you talking about?" But I'll bet your fellowship has similar imbalances of priority.

My point is even more basic: If a novice Christian can "mess up" the communion of "mature" Christians by forgetting a "pause," then somebody is missing the main thing in the Lord's Supper!

Some people say they can't sing praises if the song is not an old hymn, or if it is on an overhead, or because some other worshipers are lifting their hands or clapping along. But this is ridiculous. None of these "requirements of a praise atmosphere" have any sacred origin whatsoever! If those requirements have to be met for someone to praise God, then they are missing the main thing and not imitating the heart of heaven.

Some people complain that they can't get anything out of the worship because some songs are too slow, or some are too fast, or the guy leading the prayer marks time with a calendar. We are missing the point again!

Captain Gerald Coffee, POW for seven years in North Vietnam, spoke of his "comrades in those various cells and cell blocks in prison, men upon whom I depended and who in turn depended upon me, sometimes desperately."[10] Their call to worship on Sundays was a series of taps on the walls of their cells. The prayers and Scriptures they exchanged were not even verbal, yet they worshiped. Their priority was reflecting the heart of God to each other.

The heart of the matter is impacting the world by imitating the model of heaven. This most certainly includes learning and living his priorities. Every command ever given bows in submission to, and finds its meaning in, the greatest of all commands—to love God and each other.

Churches that exalt the heart of Christ will see commitment, morality, ethics, and outreach at levels they never thought possible. There is no greater motivation than love. Contemporary secular lyricist, Bob Seger, captures the essence of the emptiness the world feels in his song, "The Fire Inside." The selected portion below echoes the desperation and lonliness of those who seek in vain to satisfy the "fire inside."

> The darkness scatters as the lights flash on
> They hold one another just a little too long
> And they move apart and then move on
>
> On to the street, on to the next
> Safe in the knowledge that they tried
> Faking the smile, hiding the pain
> Never satisfied
> The fire inside
> Fire inside

Like wind on the plains, sand through the glass
Waves rolling in with the tide
Dreams die hard and we watch them erode
But we cannot be denied
The fire inside[11]

The message is clear: something is burning within us that keeps trying to find satisfaction.

Unpredictable emotions. Brokenness. Frustration. Loneliness. The world is longing to find substance. Someone who knows what is important. Someone who is stable and can offer true love. Is anyone on earth more equipped to answer their deepest needs than those who represent the heart of heaven?

During my first year in college, I began this private, yet desperate, search to see if anyone had what I was looking for. A fire inside was burning, and this fire led me to investigate the God written about in the Bible. I decided to ask Jesus to become my life manager, immediately taking over all operations.

As I began seeking to know him, I had much to unlearn, but it wasn't long until spiritual changes became evident in my life. Not all of my friends and acquaintances applauded. Their snubs and snickers shook me for a time, and doubts lingered. At times

Is anyone on earth more equipped to answer their deepest needs than those who represent the heart of heaven?

this caused me to wonder if trading in the generational pattern to which I had submitted for over twenty years was really a decision I could live with.

One conversation with a childhood acquaintance brought clarity to it all. Leaning against our cars in a parking lot, he spent two hours lamenting his life and the futility of even trying to *get ahead*. Then he asked me what I was up to. With butterflies flapping in my stomach to the pounding of my heart, I recounted my conversion to Christ. He interrupted, smirking a cynical, "You gotta be jokin' me. What in the h____ are you thinking? Are you kissing up to your parents for something? Why'd you go and do a stupid thing like that!"

As his barrage of questions attempted to blast holes in my faith, I unexpectedly felt *anchored* and *empowered*. With humility, confidence, and an unfamiliar love for him, I simply replied, "Because I was as sad and demoralized then as you are now, and I didn't have it in me to keep up the charade."

Tears filled his eyes as they shifted toward a rock he was nudging with his foot. He shuffled to his car to leave. I think he had to. From low in his seat, his longing eyes connected with mine for the last time. He said, "Donny, don't turn back. You're the only one of us who made it."

We both knew exactly what he meant. He was not talking houses, careers, or status. He was talking life. He *believes* in God. I am *experiencing* God. The difference is immeasurable.

The harsh realities of life can leave us in a dark depression and private pessimism, even if we have always believed there is a God. Instead of turning toward him, we become bitterly disappointed in him or we lie about how we really feel. Distance is the result either way.

Why is just believing there is a God not enough? The only way God can affect the mainstream of our lives is for us to include him intimately in our daily thoughts, feelings, and actions. This latter approach leads to serene optimism, a quiet boldness, and a heart secured by faith in his perfect wisdom and undivided allegiance to our relationship.

He *believes* in God. I am *experiencing* God. The difference is immeasurable.

Heaven in your real world comes like each new breath of oxygen: you have to take it in before it can give you life. Imitating Jesus begins with learning his ways. But the empowering experience comes with action—bringing his touch to another person, reflecting his eyes, sounding his tones, demonstrating his heart.

Embracing
Heaven's
Methods

*Maturity
through
Hardship*

Part Three Prelude

"I believe, help my unbelief."[1] The father of a demon-possessed boy spoke these words out loud to Jesus, but almost all of us have whispered them in our hearts at one time or another. Perhaps the most famous doubter is the apostle we have renamed Doubting Thomas. Truth be known, we probably ought to confess him to be Honest Thomas, for he certainly shares the struggle of our generation to come to faith in things unseen.

So far in this book, we have explored two steps to experiencing the transforming power of heaven in our real world: accepting the message of heaven, and imitating the model of heaven. But what do you do when you get the props knocked out from under your faith? How do you deal with the dashed expectations and lingering doubts that God is as caring as he proclaims?

In this final section, we will study four key difficulties people of all generations face. We will set them in the biblical framework of heaven's method of maturing us. I believe that a few hints as to what God is doing through the pain, testing, confrontations, and servanthood he calls us to will go a long way toward helping us see heaven at work in our hardships.

I faced this battle with new intensity in watching one of my children come to faith. Children are individuals. Discovering their differences was fun when they were young and we were new parents. We joked often about which child, or childish behavior, was reflecting the *other* parent. But individuality and independence are not the same thing, and two years ago, the process of coming to faith in our oldest son introduced us to his *eternal independence.*

My wife discreetly intercepted me at the door one evening as I came in from work. "Bub needs to talk to you," she said. From our eleven-year partnership at the time, I could read the tone of her voice: this was not an emergency, but it was critical.

Gently tapping on our oldest son's open door, I noticed a slight shifting in his eyes when I entered. Trying to put him at ease, I asked, "What's on your mind, Buddy?"

"I've got something to tell you, Dad. *I am having trouble believing in God.*"

For his nine years, this was big. The biggest. His eyes scanned my face for any sign. I just hugged him. My son is not me, and in so many ways we are all thankful for that. At this moment, however, his God-created independence was sobering.

After a moment of embrace, his arms began relaxing, and I knew he needed me to speak. Only heaven's words would do. "Bub," I said, "I've never been more proud of you than I am tonight."

Stunned by my words, I could almost hear the gears grinding in his mind, attempting to reconcile his *confession* with my *profession*. He was thinking to himself, "I just said I'm not convinced of the God I hear my dad proclaim in every public and private arena of our lives, yet he said he is proud of me!"

His face communicated his confusion, so I continued, "Bub, I can take you to Sunday school, Christian camps, youth rallies, and home Bible studies, but *I can't take you to heaven.*"

My voice cracked. "Only your faith in Jesus can get you to heaven, and until you ask your own questions and get your own answers, you will never have your own faith."

This was big—for me too. Two roads, and even God would not force him to choose heaven. My immense affection for my firstborn son could not get him one inch closer to heaven.

He understood. "What made you believe, Dad?" (*Now that was a question I could answer.*) "Many things," I replied. "Would you like to talk

> "Until you ask your own ques- tions and get your own answers, you will never have your own faith."

about it?" "Not tonight," he yawned, "but how about in our devotional?"

Our family gathers for a faith-building family night once a week, so I agreed we would dedicate the devotional that week to evidences for faith.

We discussed the wonders of creation—birds and bees, elephants and emperor penguins, matter, atoms, and the human body. We moved on to the miracle of having the Bible and the miracle of lives transformed by its message. We each shared our favorite stories from the life of Jesus and then closed by recalling miraculous answers to prayers we have witnessed with our own eyes. I could see a budding belief radiate from his captivated soul.

He was coming to faith. His smile was about to jump right off his face, so I asked him to lead a prayer to close the devotional. Here is his exact prayer: "Dear God. You are so great. You knew some people would believe right away and others would need *hints along the way.* Thank you for the hints along the way. Amen."

That moment in parenting has been equaled, but never surpassed. Watching the invisible God create visible faith in a human spirit, especially my firstborn, perhaps did more for my faith than his.

Is faith possible for you? I mean a deeper faith—a focused faith. A faith propped up only by God himself and not by circumstances or the fulfillment of the script of your expectations? I pray this last section will provide some of the hints you're looking for.

9
Maturing through Pain

Committing When You Feel Like Quitting

I met Abram, an international student pursuing his doctorate in genetics, at a campus retreat. Through the course of our conversation, he told me of his engagement to marry when he returned to South Africa. I surmised out loud that it must be tough to be so far away from his fiancée. He assured me that the dating and engagement rituals in his home country were so different from ours that it would require some explanation. Although his one-hour description of the marriage traditions was riveting, the entire process boiled down to this profound *result* and *statement*. Result: The divorce rate among his people is about 1 percent (compared to 53 percent in the U.S.). Statement: "In

115

America," he said, "you are committed to those you love. Among my people, you love those you are committed to."

Is there a difference beyond the semantics? I believe so. In his view of relationships, you are committed—no matter how you *feel*. Thus, the commitment carries the relationship. This is actually a description of the *agape* love described in the Bible—the kind of love God teaches his children, the kind of love where commitment can coexist with difficulty, differences, discipline—even hurt.

No one loves those who hurt him with more maturity than God himself. God experienced hurt from the very beginning of his relationship with Israel. Through his undying love, in spite of the pain they heaped upon him, God taught the difference between the conditional and temporary love of this earth and the mature love of heaven.

God's Wedding

Even Cecil B. deMille couldn't match the awesome description in Exodus 19–34 of God descending to meet with his people on Mount Sinai. The earth literally quaked and trembled when heaven came to the real world.

The purpose of the Sinai visit was twofold: God came as the *groom* in the wedding ceremony to seal a lasting covenant with his bride, Israel. He also came to proclaim the *laws* that would serve as a guide for their marriage. When the God of heaven married his people on earth, he made it clear that their relationship would bring about changes in their lives. Join me at the ceremony.

Then Moses went up to God, and the Lord called to him from the mountain and said, "This is what you are to say to the house of Jacob and what you are to tell the people of Israel: 'You yourselves have seen what I did to Egypt, and how I carried you on eagles' wings and brought you to myself. Now if you obey me fully and keep my covenant, then out of all the nations you will be my treasured possession. Although the whole earth is mine, you will be for me a kingdom of priests and a holy nation.'"

So Moses went back and summoned the elders of the people and set before them all the words the Lord had commanded him to speak. The people all responded together, *"We will do everything the Lord has said."*

And the Lord said to Moses, "Go to the people and consecrate them today and tomorrow. Have them wash their clothes and be ready by the third day, because on that day the Lord will come down on Mount Sinai."[1]

This sounds like a courtship, proposal, and invitation to the wedding!

Weddings are special, and sometimes comical. One especially sticks out in my mind. The young couple seemed particularly well suited to each other. The wedding itself was rather extravagant by the standards of our small, southeast Ohio town. Certainly, it was the event of the summer, as the full house demonstrated. No one who was anyone was going to miss it.

Everything was picture perfect. The penguin-suited groomsmen escorted their beautiful belles down the aisle to their pedestal of pageantry. As the mother rose to signal the entrance of the queen of this processional, all stood and adoringly welcomed her with the appropriately muffled *oohs* and *ahhs*.

The ceremony began . . .

"Dearly beloved, we are gathered here today . . ."

"Do you take this man to be your lawfully wedded . . ?"

"With this ring, I thee wed . . ."

Everything was going as smooth as silk. Then, in my peripheral vision, I noticed that the bride and groom's candles on either side of the unity candle were not lit. We were at the part of the ceremony where the bride and groom were to pick up the two smaller, lit candles and jointly light the larger unity candle in the middle. This was to be followed by an extinguishing of the two smaller candles, thus signifying their lifelong union.

Believe me, the middle of a wedding ceremony is a tough place to improvise; however, I had to keep it moving as gracefully as possible. As the bride finished repeating her ring vows, I leaned over toward the best man with minimal movement and gently whispered, "Do you have a match or lighter?"

No one in the audience—or even the bride and groom—was aware there was a problem, until the best man ended their blissful ignorance with the booming reply, "I don't smoke!"

The audience became a sea of bobbing heads, flashing eyes, and straining ears. The groom's forehead started sprouting little beads of sweat, and the bride's face turned the color of her dress. (I still don't remember asking him if he smoked!)

It went from bad to worse. The ring bearer, overhearing the discussion, took off running up the aisle, yelling, "My grandpa smokes! Hey Grandpa, they need your lighter to get them candles goin'." When he returned with the Bic Butane, the bride was swaying and nervously humming a childhood tune. The groom's glassy eyes were fixed on my lapel microphone like a religious icon.

> The ring bearer took off running up the aisle, yelling, "Hey, Grandpa, they need your lighter to get them candles goin'."

I had to get order restored, so I handed the lighter to the best man and asked him to light the candles. Finishing the introduction to the unity candle ceremony, we turned around to find that he had lit all three candles, including the one they were to light. With a sigh, I blew it out.

But somehow, they got hitched: the license was signed, the ceremony saved, the candle lit, and the covenant completed. Love conquered all. I finally issued the marital proclamation: "I now pronounce you husband and wife."

After all that happened, the final announcement signaled the end of the suffering . . . I mean the ceremony; but even more than that, it stated clearly that marriage is a commitment, not a ceremony. And just as the snafus of the ceremony could not derail the wedding, so the struggles of the relationship should not undo the marriage.

What does this have to do with Mount Sinai? That mountaintop wedding ceremony was about God coming to the real world to make known his loving commitment to his people.

God's wedding also encountered a catastrophe that threatened to collapse the covenant before the vows were consummated. The ceremony had been going great. Then, God's peripheral hearing revealed trouble. According to Exodus 32, the people of Israel (his bride), who were camped at the foot of the mountain, had made a golden calf, and were worshiping it. They were already going back on their first and second vows of having no other gods and making no graven images to worship. This is the equivalent to breaking their marriage vows *during the wedding!*

What Does God's Reaction Teach Us About Mature Love?

Put yourself in God's place. What would you do? Would this be a good time for the preacher to ask, "If anyone has any reason why these two should not be wed in holy matrimony, speak now or forever hold your peace"? If we were to answer this question from the valley of humanity, the wedding would be over. But that's why we are on this mountain: God was there to teach his people a heavenly level of maturity in regard to commitments and love. And if we appreciate his example, we will better understand how we can mature in the way we face the difficulties in our relationships. What does God do, and what do we learn about him from how he handles this?

Mature love honestly reveals hurt.

First, God reveals his hurt. What do you do when someone hurts you in a relationship? Do you try to punish them indirectly, hoping they will get the picture and initiate a reconciliation? Do you implode your feelings and become silently bitter? Do you talk ill of them to everyone who has an ear? Do you take it out on some *safe target* who you subconsciously know will take it, like your small child? Which of these options actually empowers you to have better relationships? None!

Notice that God very directly stated to the Israelites that they had hurt him and that they needed to take responsibility for the damage they were causing to the relationship.

> Then the Lord said to Moses, "Go down, because your people, whom you brought up out of Egypt, have become corrupt. They have been quick to turn away from what I have commanded them and have made themselves an idol cast in the shape of a calf. They have bowed down to it and sacrificed to it and have said, 'These are your gods, O Israel, who brought you up out of Egypt.'
>
> "I have seen these people, and they are a stiff-necked people. Now leave me alone so that my anger may burn against them and that I may destroy them. Then I will make you into a great nation."[2]

Was God too hard on them? Many Americans cringe and pull away from a God such as this. All this talk about anger and destruction turns them off. Many think that expressing true feelings of hurt is an act of condemnation, blame, or an attempt to "guilt" someone into submission. At the root of this desire to avoid blame for causing hurt is ultimately an attempt to duck responsibility. In my premarital counseling, I give this rule for marriage: "If you are going to be married, you can't keep living single!"

Israel had invited another groom to the wedding and had engaged in spiritual intercourse with this other "god groom" in the middle of the wedding!

This simply means that your life is accountable to another person in every way. Mature love takes into account that when my attitudes and actions hurt another person, or when they hurt me, the hurt needs to be openly revealed.

Let's put God's situation with Israel into context. Israel had invited another groom to the wedding and had engaged in spiritual intercourse with this other "god groom" *in the middle of the wedding!* Can't we feel God's hurt, experiencing with him the reason for his intense anger?

If this happened to any of us during our wedding ceremony, we would be insane with hurt, embarrassment, and rage. I can confidently say that not a one of us would even entertain the thought of going through with the wedding.

Any attempt by someone to talk us into it would probably cost them our friendship, without qualification.

But not God. If we will stay on the mountain with him and discipline ourselves to walk with him through the entire situation, we will learn much about how God lives and interacts in our real world for our ultimate best good.

To gain some understanding of this covenant relationship God desires with us, let's digress for a moment and visit with a man named Hosea. No prophet or priest in the Old Testament better understood God's commitment to his bride than Hosea. Listen to how he describes God's love in Hosea 11:1–9.

> When Israel was a child I loved him, and out of Egypt I called my son. But the more I called Israel, the further they went from me. They sacrificed to the Baals and they burned incense to images. It was I who taught Ephraim[3] to walk, taking them by the arms, but they did not realize it was I who healed them. I led them with cords of human kindness, with ties of love; I lifted the yoke from their neck and bent down to feed them. Will they not return to Egypt and will not Assyria rule over them because they refuse to repent? Swords will flash in their cities, will destroy the bars of their gates and put an end to their plans. My people are determined to turn from me. Even if they call to the Most High, he will by no means exalt them. . . .

Does this sound like Sinai so far? Keep listening.

> How can I [God] give you up, Ephraim? How can I hand you over, Israel? How can I treat you like

Admah? How can I make you like Zeboiim?[4] My heart is changed within me; all my compassion is aroused. I will not carry out my fierce anger, nor will I turn and devastate Ephraim. For I am God, and not man—the Holy One among you. I will not come in wrath."

Mature love does not hide hurt.

God was honest about his feelings so that we can experience his pain over our sin. True relationships cannot be built on the motto: "I'm okay; you're okay," when the truth is—we're not okay. God also wants to convince us that *we too are going to be hurt* by our sin. Because of God's maturity, his love can and will endure the hurt that comes with relationships. Mature love does not hide the hurt. True love is based on the commitment that within our love we will honestly deal with hurt.

Mature love makes security a priority.

As we close the twentieth century, we are desperate for relationships that are honest but also secure. Through fourteen years of pastoral counseling, I have felt the pain of countless people who are broken. They either find they have lived in a fantasy of security, only to be smashed by an honesty that ends with a devastating good-bye; or they live in a harsh honesty that leaves them constantly in fear of when the other shoe is going to drop. God is honest, but he is also secure. God can challenge the things in our lives that must be changed in order to maintain a healthy relationship, without making us feel that any infraction would sever our ties.

Mature love allows discipline to have a healing effect.

The Exodus account continues, revealing how the wedding was saved by the love and discipline of God.

> Moses saw that the people were running wild and that Aaron had let them get out of control and so become a laughing stock to their enemies. So [Moses] stood at the entrance to the camp and said, "Whoever is for the Lord, come to me."[5]

God issued a summons, coupled with an opportunity. In essence he said, "Let's give everyone an opportunity to show their true heart and return to me." God tells us in Psalm 103 that he is like a father in his compassion: he will not harbor anger against us, and he remembers that we are people who struggle with doing what is right.

People who do not know God well often emphasize God's punishment of those who chose not to come to the Lord's side,[6] but they do not underscore the fact that a groom who was jilted in the middle of his wedding ceremony actually gave his bride an opportunity to rejoin the proceedings and be forgiven.

I find it disturbing that God's critics use a standard of judging him and his actions that, when applied to their own parenting, managing, or communication styles, would be considered unfair. These critics will not tolerate someone misquoting them in word or emphasis, yet rarely is God's whole story told. I know this firsthand, as I was in their camp for many years. I am truly sorry now for the number of people I misled in my shortsighted misrepresentation of God, even in casual conversations. How patient God has been with my uninformed and stubborn heart. I accused *him* of the imbalance that was *mine*.

When God offers his people the opportunity to turn things around, the result is very telling. The Bible says, "All the Levites rallied to him." The Levites were only one tribe out of the twelve that made up the Israelite nation. How heartbreaking to see hundreds of thousands of people, whom you saved from grueling slavery in Egypt, not only break their vows during the wedding, but reject your plea for return and forgiveness. How much can God take? The reason for the discipline that followed is so much more obvious when understood in context.

Mature love fully reconciles, following repentance.

Following the punishment of those who would not turn their lives back to the relationship, Moses set up a conference with God to see if they would proceed or if the wedding was off. (The Holy Spirit bugged the conference so we are privy to the conversation.) Moses said to the Lord,

> You have been telling me, "Lead these people," but you have not let me know who you will send with me. You have said, "I know you by name and you have found favor with me." If you are pleased with me, teach me your ways so I may know you and con-

tinue to find favor with you. Remember that this nation is your people.

The Lord replied, "My Presence will go with you, and I will give you rest." . . . And the Lord said, "I will cause all my goodness to pass in front of you, and I will proclaim my name, the Lord, in your presence. I will have mercy on whom I will have mercy, and I will have compassion on whom I will have compassion." . . . And he passed in front of Moses, proclaiming, "The Lord, the Lord, the compassionate and gracious God, slow to anger, abounding in love and faithfulness, maintaining love to thousands, and forgiving wickedness, rebellion and sin. Yet he does not leave the guilty unpunished. . . ."

Moses bowed to the ground at once and worshiped. "O Lord, if I have found favor in your eyes," he said, "then let the Lord go with us. Although this is a stiff-necked people, forgive our wickedness and our sin, and take us as your inheritance."

Then the Lord said: "I am making a covenant with you. Before all your people I will do wonders never before done in any nation in all the world. The people you live among will see how awesome is the work that I, the Lord will do for you."[7]

Wow! The vows are up, and they're good. Love conquers all. The covenant was sealed and the proclamation announced: God is in love with us, and wants to take us for his own. This is what the mature love of God is all about.

What Does the Life of Christ Teach Us about Mature Love?

Jesus demonstrated this same love at Calvary. Listen in on two profound conversations from the crosses of Calvary.

> Two other men, both criminals, were also led out with him to be executed. When they came to the place called the Skull, there they crucified him, along with the criminals—one on his right, the other on his left. Jesus said, "Father, forgive them, for they do not know what they are doing."[8]

> Those who passed by hurled insults at him, shaking their heads. . . .
> In the same way the chief priests and teachers of the law mocked him among themselves. . . . Those crucified with him also heaped insults on him.[9]

> One of the criminals who hung there hurled insults at him: "Aren't you the Christ? Save yourself and us!"
> But the other criminal rebuked him. "Don't you fear God," he said, "since you are under the same sentence? We are punished justly, for we are getting what we deserve. But this man has done nothing wrong."
> Then he said, "Jesus, remember me when you come into your kingdom."
> Jesus answered him, "I tell you the truth, today you will be with me in paradise."[10]

Both Sinai and Calvary reveal the changeless desire of the heart of God to *make love stick even through the hurt.* Although many, including *both* criminals, started out rejecting the reconciling sacrifice of Jesus, his offer of forgiveness moved one criminal to repentance and salvation.

God loves us, and he is not surprised by our sin. For the good of our relationship, however, he will not let our unfaithfulness and offenses go unchallenged. Heaven's love is modeled at Sinai and Calvary.

> Both Sinai and Calvary reveal the changeless desire of the heart of God to *make love stick even through the hurt.*

What Can We Do to Improve Our Relationships Right Now?

Heaven in the real world offers us the insight and power to change every relationship in our lives. Heaven's love declares that relationships can, and should, be honest and secure. Truth and true feelings can be shared. Discipline and reconciliation can take place. Those who appreciate the way God can use these difficulties to mature them in their love will experience a level of friendship and intimacy that can only be described as heavenly.

How does this translate into our relationships? It gives us the courage and heart to share our hurts while managing our emotions. It gives us the strength to step into someone's

life and bring to light something that will hurt them and
their relationships without resorting to implosions, explo-
sions, or ultimatums. Here are two steps learned at the front
line of relationship building.

Turn on the A. C. (Accurate Communication).

Heaven's mature love opens endless relationship possibilities. Often times, we are looking for a way to state a dis-
agreement or hurt without giving the impression that we are
putting the relationship on the line. One statement that has
proved very helpful is, "I may be confused about how I feel
about what we are discussing, but I am not confused about
how I feel about you. I love you and I always will." This
simple statement opens the door to expressing the point of
conflict without adding the emotional anxiety of possibly
losing the relationship.

Turn down the heat!

I have heard so many people make the comment, "I'm
just hot tempered." Or, "I have a short fuse." Or, "I just blow
up. It's just the way I am." I must confess that very few
statements reveal more obvious immaturity than these.
There is only one Great I AM, and that is God! The rest of us
are the "I am becoming." If you are hot tempered, *get over it
through the power of Jesus!* You are ruining your relationships
through both your angry outbursts and your immaturity in
not seriously committing yourself to deal with it.

This awful truth was brought home to me through a
conversation with my wife Susan. We both have very strong

emotions, but I had very poor anger management skills. This included such famous moments in our early marriage as me punching a hole in the drywall of our home.

As we were driving one afternoon, Susan was expressing truth to me in a loving way, but I was feeling furious inside. I knew that my normal reaction to any conversation like this was explosion, and I knew that exploding was unacceptable. It just isn't productive to act like that. Then the Lord's examples of Sinai and Calvary came to me with the following words, which I shared with Susan.

"Susan, I want to tell you how I feel." (I could hardly believe the quiet and calm tone of voice with which I was responding.) I continued, "Right now I'm so angry with you I can't even think straight. All I can think of is what I'm going to say back at you. But I want you to know, I don't agree with my feelings. Although these are my true feelings, they're not based on truth, and I'm in sin. I don't feel justified to have this rage in my heart, but it's still there. I want you to know I'm sorry, and I believe I'm wrong."

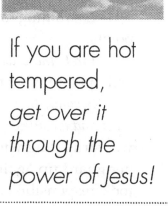

If you are hot tempered, get over it through the power of Jesus!

Never before in five years of marriage had a confrontational conversation come out like this! But we were learning to honestly express hurt in a secure and controlled way.

"I know this is a very important conversation," I continued, "but I can't respond right now. If I do, I will fail. I need some time to repent. If you can give me a few hours to get my feelings under the management of the Spirit of love, I will be fine. I promise you I will restart this conversation later today. You do not have to walk around on eggshells, wondering if I'm still mad. I will initiate this time of sharing when it's convenient for you."

Susan began to cry. I was confused until she explained. "Thank you so much for sharing your true feelings in an honest and calm way. I didn't understand how the things I was sharing with you were affecting your feelings." Later that evening we returned to the conversation in a fresh way, and it was as if our marriage was reborn. Since we submitted our love to the maturing work of God, our marriage has been so different.

Examining our conversation, there were three keys points.

First, there was honesty in security. We were both calm and open to what each other felt.

Second, there was an open admission of the wrong in my heart and a confession of sin. Susan felt secure that, although I was struggling with sinful feelings, she didn't have to keep her guard up against continuing out-of-control responses. I took responsibility; so she didn't have to. When someone admits to their own sin, it makes a strong statement of dedication to the permanence of the relationship. Face it: many of our *true* feelings are not *based* on truth. What she was saying was true, but my feelings were not a balanced reflection of what she was saying. I was blowing it out of proportion, and that was a sinful, manipulative lifestyle I had learned. No excuses. No rationalizations. I sinned. I was wrong. I was sorry.

Third, there was a verbal commitment to the ongoing of the relationship. This assured Susan that she could speak the truth to me about her feelings and observations without having to fear that it would severely or permanently wound our relationship. Had she not exercised so much patience, I would have potentially continued to wound the relationship without learning how to alter my actions.

God is calling us from Sinai and Calvary to trade in our combative tantrums and ultimatums for a mature love that accurately and securely expresses hurts without holding the relationship hostage. The next time you find yourself looking for little reasons to cut someone out of your circle of love, make a trip to the summit of Sinai or the foot of Calvary, and stay there until you can come down and proclaim your covenant of love once again. God forgave a bride who broke her vows before the ceremony was even over, because he wanted her. Jesus forgave the lying lynch mob that hung him on trumped-up charges, because his desire to save them knew no limits, even death.

Covenants are not based on profit sharing. Covenants are born in individual hearts when they decide to do what is best for others, no matter what it costs them or what response they receive. If the person needs us to sacrifice, we will. If they need discipline, we give it firmly with love. If they need to hurt for their sin, we let them hurt, but with a watchful eye so that they will not be overwhelmed by excessive sorrow when they repent.

Since everyone needs reassurance and love, covenant people learn the best way to give it to the people in their lives, and they offer it generously. When others do not fit our patterns or fulfill our expectations, we choose to examine ourselves instead of accusing them. We are rarely caught putting others down, and when we are, we quickly repent—retracing our trail of malicious talk, confessing our sin, and restoring their honor.

The phrase, "no pain, no gain" is nowhere more true than in the methods God uses to mature us in love. And only when we truly love someone who has hurt and wronged us will we even get a taste of how we affect God.

10 Maturing through Testing

Standing Firm When You Feel Blown Away

When our college-age friend Robin called home, her voice was filled with even more enthusiasm than her normal hyper self. She had found the man she was going to marry. Rattling on about this wonderful guy, she asked if I would perform their wedding. I was overjoyed for her and assured her I would consider it a privilege.

I finally met Damon, and he is amazing. He is an Eagle Scout, an accomplished mountain climber, and a dedicated Christian. But at the first premarital counseling session, I noticed one minor item Robin had left out: Damon's right arm was severed just below the shoulder. I learned that it happened in a car accident when he was very young. It didn't matter, of course, and he was obviously not letting this setback determine the attitude or altitude of his life.

Then at the wedding, I met his dad and mom. Upon meeting his father, a very successful inventor and vendor of prosthetics, I was more than intrigued to discover that his *left* arm was severed just below the shoulder. He had been involved in an accident with explosives when he was a young boy. Two in the same family!

At the reception I learned more details about their lives through a conversation with Damon's mother, a devoted and exuberant Christian woman. I asked her how she dealt with Damon's loss since she had already had to face that same tragedy with her husband. Her reply could spawn a book by itself.

> "Although I am not thankful that the accident happened, I am very thankful that it happened in our family, because we were so prepared to handle it."

She said, "Although I am not thankful that the accident happened, I am very thankful that it happened in our family, because we were so prepared to handle it."

Wow! Instead of complaining of the unfairness or harboring ill will toward God for not spreading the difficulty around, she saw their earlier testing as preparation for things that were to come later in their life. Heaven used testing as a method of maturing her for what she would face in her real world.

I saw this same spirit on a giant, bold sign on the side of a bombed-out church building next door to the crater left by the April 19, 1995, bombing of the Murrah Federal Building in Oklahoma City. In red block letters emblazoned on a pure white background it read simply, "God Reigns, and We Will Remain!"

These believers reflect the spirit James was attempting to instill in us with his admonition concerning suffering and maturity.

> Consider it pure joy, my brothers, whenever you face trials of many kinds, because you know that the testing of your faith develops perseverance. Perseverance must finish its work so that you may be mature and complete, not lacking anything.[1]

God's process of maturity includes testing and preparation. We rarely consider that every hardship is a testing ground to prepare us for destinations that lie in our future. Jesus told us that "whoever can be trusted with very little can be trusted with much." In order for testing to have its maturing effect on our lives, we must *embrace* it—not *fight* it. This is a difficult concept, but the Bible provides us with examples and teachings to empower us.

Genesis 22 shares the most powerful example of testing, outside the life of Christ, found anywhere in Scripture:

> Some time later God tested Abraham. He said to him, "Abraham!"
> "Here I am," he replied.

> Then God said, "Take your son, your only son,
> Isaac, whom you love, and go to the region of Moriah.
> Sacrifice him there as a burnt offering on one of the
> mountains I will tell you about."[2]

Wow. Have you ever answered the phone and wished you hadn't? Can you imagine getting a call from God? I don't mean a heavenly telemarketing call from Quality Control or Accounting. I mean a person-to-person call from God himself!

But what would you think after you heard why he was calling? "My son? You want me to do *what* with my only son?" Some who read this with twentieth-century eyes come away angry with God. They criticize him as being dictatorial, unreasonable, or maybe sadistic. But what do you say we give Abraham an opportunity to tell us how he viewed God's request and what the whole situation meant to him. We can learn from Abraham how to stand firm when we feel blown away—and how to actually *mature* through testing.

Learn to Reason by Faith

Hebrews 11:17–19 gives us an overall view after the fact. Take a moment and read with a detective's eye, looking for hints as to what was going through Abraham's mind.

> *By faith* Abraham, when God tested him, offered Isaac
> as a sacrifice. He who had received the promises was
> about to sacrifice his one and only son, even though
> God had said to him, "It is through Isaac that your off-
> spring will be reckoned." Abraham *reasoned* that God

could raise the dead, and figuratively speaking, he did receive Isaac back from death.

Here's the key: Abraham *reasoned by faith*. He refused to use worldly reasoning to understand what God can do or is doing in our lives. Abraham believed that God would provide even before he saw the provision. I believe that part of the reason Abraham received the *provision* of the Lord was that he was committed to doing the will of the Lord. He believed God would never lead him where he would not provide for him. God had promised to bring a great nation through Isaac, so Abraham just believed he would; even if that meant raising Isaac from the dead.

Christians are filled with the powerful Spirit of God, who leads us to do seemingly impossible things by his supernatural power. Abraham and Sarah had baby Isaac when their bodies were old and as good as dead.[3] Abraham had lived in the presence of God. This lifestyle enlarged Abraham's faith in preparation for the coming test—and his faith was *enlarged in direct proportion to the size of the test he was about to encounter.*

Notice for a moment how this principle was applied even by Jesus in his life on earth. Matthew 4:1–11 relates the account of Jesus' temptation in the wilderness. The trio of temptations closed on a high mountain, where Satan showed Jesus all the kingdoms of the earth and their splendor. The deal Satan offered Jesus must have been tough to pass up. Since the goal of Christ's work was to make "the kingdom of the world become the kingdom of our Lord and of his Christ,"[4] Satan tried to convince Jesus that he could bypass the painful parts of the plan and still accomplish his goal. But this was a test.

When Satan tempts us, he doesn't come right out and scream, "God is dead! He hates you, and you are a loser, and you are going to hell to burn with me forever!" (That comes after he has already crushed someone.) His tactics are not so obvious. He simply tries to divert us from our spiritual reasoning and our faith.

When tempting Jesus, Satan did not try to convince him that he was not the Son of God. Instead, Satan tried to get Jesus to abandon his spiritual reasoning, and thus rebel against God's plan for his life. Satan used the same selfish desires that drove him to rebel in heaven to tempt Jesus. Satan's success would come to the surface only if he could get Jesus to live for the victories he could see, hear, and touch.

But Jesus didn't bite! He could see right through Satan's lies, and he simply told Satan what Satan already knew, "It is written: Worship the Lord your God, and serve him only."[5] The Greek words for "worship" and "serve" used in his reply are both associated with the singular lifestyle of reverence that causes us to offer ourselves to God as living sacrifices—not conforming to the pattern of the world, but being transformed by the renewing of our minds so we can prove what the will of God is.[6] Jesus kept his spiritual eyes focused on the prize that lay at the end of the road of faith.

Abraham and Jesus both underscore the fact that *faith reasoning* changes how we live in the present and affects us in the future.

We believe Romans 8:28: "In all things God works for the good of those who love him, who have been called according to his purpose." But this passage of Scripture does not mean that God, in any way, *caused* anyone to abuse you or me. "God takes no pleasure in the death of anyone,"[7] and that includes the special one whom you may be mourning. "God cannot be tempted by evil, nor does he tempt anyone,"[8] and that includes our loved ones who are in trouble with drugs, alcohol, and the law. It isn't God who breaks up families through painful divorces; God "hates divorce," just as much as you do.[9]

What Romans 8:28 does mean is that Satan is limited in what he can do to us and that whatever pain Satan brings to our lives, God will bring good out of it. Satan will have no victory! It is Satan who comes to "steal, kill, and destroy," but it is God who came to our real world to give us life. Our understanding of these truths will grow as we learn to *reason by faith*.

Trust God to Pack Your Bags

The first time I took an international trip, my packing partner was an experienced world traveler. He came to the house to go over the packing with me. I had already begun filling the suitcase with the items I thought we would need. He quickly dumped more than half of my things out, and then began to tell me what was necessary. Although I questioned him and was sure he had thrown out some essential items, his experience proved precise. In fifteen days of

Middle East travel, I had exactly what I needed and nothing extra.

God knows the journey we are taking; therefore, he also knows exactly what we need to be prepared for what lies ahead. Many people continually question what God has allowed to happen in their lives, rarely stopping to ask what God was planning on doing with these things later on.

The ultimate faith destroyer in the midst of testing is the "I don't deserve this" syndrome. We think that our identity and station in life deserve certain returns, results, and rewards. When these expectations go unfulfilled, and we are faced with hard times and heartaches, we often view what we have experienced as negative baggage. And since we do not believe these trials should have been in our lives in the first place, we go about trying to get rid of the negative baggage.

> The ultimate faith destroyer in the midst of testing is the "I don't deserve this" syndrome.

Instead of getting rid of our negative baggage, let's simply bring it to God and say, "God, here is what Satan has done, and he is still using it to hurt me. I want you to look over my baggage, heal it, mend it, file it, rearrange it, and give it back to me with a commission. Anoint me a messenger of hope to others who have been wounded. Give me the strength to believe in your power, no matter how big the test seems, so that I can honestly be one who has witnessed your ability to provide for me."

God knows better than you or me what we need packed into our spiritual, emotional, mental, and experiential bags for the journey ahead. We must resist the temptation to sidestep the testing in our paths, because our current tests will bring the maturity we will need to endure future testing.

Act on Your Faith One Step at a Time

Testing is a stair-step process that enables us to grow in the resources we will need for opportunities and difficulties of life. If we are not willing to be committed to God in the small tests, we're actually short-circuiting his plan to prepare us for the tests he knows lie in our future.

How do we begin building a commitment to God that will sustain us through any test? How can we stand firm through the storm so that we can eventually enjoy God's provision? Let's go back to Genesis 22 and walk with Abraham and Isaac to Mount Moriah. "Early the next morning Abraham *got up* and *saddled his donkey.* He took with him two of his servants and his son Isaac. When he had *cut enough wood* for the burnt offering, he *set out* for the place God had told him about."[10]

The way we bring our commitment to God to the level needed to endure the tests is *one step at a time.* This one verse in Genesis is teeming with crucial, systematic steps of discipleship. The first thing that catches my attention is that Abraham *got up.* Ninety percent of success is showing up, and Abraham decided that putting off the call of God was fruitless. He didn't have it all figured out, but he went ahead and took that first step—he got up. He refused to become a victim of paralysis by analysis. He knew the first step, and he took it.

> God's provision is not like a life insurance policy where the money all comes at once at the end of the road. God's provision is like a pure mountain stream that brings just the right amount of water all along the journey

For you, it may be a first prayer (or a first-time-in-a-long-time prayer). It may be calling a spiritual friend and having a conversation about your test. It may be scouring a concordance for scriptural principles and examples of your specific test. It may be asking God to forgive you and get you back into his family. Take a first step today.

God provides so much for those who simply act on faith. After taking that first step, Abraham forged ahead in steps that increased his investment in God's way of facing the test. He saddled the donkey, he chose the servants, and he even chopped the wood.

Difficult? Yes! But step by step, Abraham was acting on his faith. How would he climb the mountain if he didn't first get out of bed? What strength would he have for the sacrifice if he couldn't even chop the wood? We must learn the connection between faithfulness in small things and the strength to handle the big things.

The test in verse 2 (of Genesis 22), and Abraham's obedience in verse 3, are nearly an exact replica of the very first call God gave Abraham (then Abram), recorded in Genesis 12:1: "The Lord had said to Abram, 'Leave your country, your people and your father's household and go to the land I will show you.' "

Had Abram not been willing to leave his home and go to a strange land, how would he ever get to the place where God would call him to sacrifice his own son? Commitment requires movement toward the place God calls us to, even if it is in incremental steps. God's provision is not like a life insurance policy where the money all comes at once at the end of the road. God's provision is like a pure mountain stream that brings just the right amount of water all along the journey.

Speak Positively about the Provision of the Lord

Tests normally get more difficult before they get easier. Many people take lightly the power of their own statements, positive or negative. Psycholinguistics is the study of self-talk. This study reveals that when you say something out loud, it has a triple effect on you. First, your mind generates the thought; second, your mouth makes the sound; third, your ears process what you said—a threefold reinforcement. Positive or negative, what is your pattern? If Zig Ziglar is correct when he says that "Attitude more than aptitude determines your altitude," and your own speech reinforces it three times, it is vital that you speak positively of the provision of God in testing.

Abraham understood this principle and spoke positively about the provision of the Lord. After Abraham and Isaac left the servants at the foot of the mountain, the journey became even more difficult. It was just the two of them, now, and their personal burdens were a little heavier. Isaac was carrying the heavy wood, and Abraham was carrying a heavy heart. Notice the progression of the conversation.

> When you say something out loud, it has a "triple effect" on you.

Isaac spoke up, "Father?"

As a father myself, I know that just that interrogative tone would cause the tears to well up in my eyes. Abraham knew the questions were coming. Why the trip? Why so early in the morning? Why so far? All the questions children ask. Why the quietness? Why do you look at me so long with those penetrating eyes?

"Yes, my son?" Abraham replied.

"The fire and the wood are here," Isaac said, "but where is the lamb for the burnt offering?"

Because Abraham was a righteous father who practiced his discipleship in the presence of his family, sacrificing to God was familiar to young Isaac. But now Isaac was about to learn the deeper meaning of giving yourself and your possessions as a sacrifice to God.

Abraham's answer spoke positively of God's provisions: "God himself will provide the lamb for the burnt offering, my son." And the two of them went on together. This statement was true in three ways. God had already provided Isaac to Abraham and Sarah in a miraculous way.[11] God would provide for the promise of making Abraham a great nation through Isaac, even if he had to raise Isaac from the dead. And God would provide a physical lamb to complete the sacrifice at the appropriate time. It was this commitment that gave Abraham the faith to speak positively to the two servants they left behind, "I and the boy will go over there. We will worship and then we will come back to you."

Notice that each time Abraham spoke to anyone about the testing, he verbally reaffirmed to them and himself that God would provide. A professor of mine, Dr. Jerry Jones, used to say, "The will of God will not lead you where the power of God cannot keep you." Heaven in the real world means speaking this assurance to others: *With the test, God will provide a way of escape so that we may endure it.*

Follow through with Absolute Obedience

Only one hundred percent will do when one hundred percent is required.

> When they reached the place God had told him about [Mount Moriah], Abraham built an altar there and arranged the wood on it. He bound his son Isaac and laid him on the altar, on top of the wood. Then he

reached out his hand and took the knife to slay his son. But the angel of the Lord called out to him from heaven, "Abraham! Abraham!"

"Here I am," he replied.

"Do not lay a hand on the boy," he said. Do not do anything to him. Now I know that you fear God, because you have not withheld from me your son, your only son."[12]

What does this teach us about the tests in our lives? It teaches us to follow through in our obedience to God, no matter where that obedience leads. Build your altar, one stone at a time. Arrange the wood. Bind the child. Grasp the knife. Raise the hand. Proceed step by step to the very end: this is how believers in God live, and this is how they experience the provision of God. Period! There is no substitute for simple obedience. Knowledge may challenge your mind, but obedience is what changes history. Abraham's own life would have been richly blessed upon hearing the voice from heaven, but all

> Knowledge may challenge your mind, but obedience is what changes history.

mankind was blessed when he *walked in the steps* of heaven.

If Abraham struggled with responding to the voice of heaven the first time, probably no sound was more welcome than when the angel called his name the second time. This time, the message was entirely altered. The angel emphatically commanded Abraham to stop the proceedings and learn the purpose of this gut-wrenching test: " 'Now I know that you fear God, because you have not withheld from me your son, your only son.' Abraham looked up and there in a thicket he saw a ram caught by its horns. He went over and took the ram and sacrificed it as a burnt offering instead of his son."[13]

The word "fear" in the phrase, "I know that you fear God," carries the sense of a *reverential trust* in God that includes commitment to his revealed will (Word). God is not training Abraham, or any of us, to be *afraid* of him. Rather, he wants a deep reverential trust to take root in our hearts so that we can obey him, even when we are afraid, even when we are tempted to turn from his will in the midst of a test.

Abraham's future was filled with opportunities—and so is ours. And, like Abraham, we do not know what they are or when they will knock. I often wonder how many possibilities have already passed me by because I was not prepared for them. Abraham witnessed more of heaven in this one episode than many people experience in a lifetime. One step at a time, he drew closer and closer to God's exact calling, and it resulted in an angel visit, an object lesson in commitment that Isaac would never forget, and the simple provision of the ram that God placed in the thicket. The text goes on to say,

> So Abraham called that place, The Lord Will Provide. And to this day it is said, "On the mountain of the Lord it will be provided." And the angel of the Lord called to Abraham from heaven a second time and said, "I swear by myself, declares the Lord, that because you have done this and have not withheld

your son, your only son, I will surely bless you and make your descendants as numerous as the stars in the sky and as the sand on the seashore. Your descendants will take possession of the cities of their enemies, and through your offspring all nations on earth will be blessed, because you have obeyed me."[14]

While visiting Mount Calvary on a trip to Israel in 1990, my eyes were streaming tears as I envisioned Jesus, our sacrificial Lamb, hanging there at the foot of the Skull. But I was almost struck numb when I turned and realized that directly behind me was the place where heaven provided a sacrificial lamb to take the place of Abraham's only son.

God wants to develop you into a mountain of spiritual maturity.

Jesus is the Lamb that saved Isaac, Abraham, you, and me; he is the Lamb of God; he is God's Son, his only Son, the Son he loves. Two thousand years after Isaac's life and Abraham's heart were spared on Mount Moriah, God's Son was crucified and his heart was crushed—on the very same mountain. Yet heaven's commitment to us was honored, glorified, and rewarded by the provision of salvation.

Abraham was told that *obedience* in his testing would bring him a blessing. That day, the blessing was the continued life and presence of his only son, Isaac. In the years and centuries to come, it meant the freeing of Israel from slavery in Egypt and the inheritance of the Promised Land. Twenty centuries later, it meant the blessing of eternal salvation for all mankind through the death of the Son of heaven.

God wants to develop you into a mountain of spiritual maturity too. That mountain is made up of thousands of stones of testing. Each of these stones has dual potential. Satan intends to use them to begin a spiritual avalanche that will send you careening into his abyss. God, however, can and will use those same *test-stones* as building blocks from heaven to form you into a bulwark of spiritual strength.

Heaven's provision in our real world is always available at higher levels than we need or use. Please meditate on the following passages of provision.

> Now to him who is able to do immeasurably more than all we ask or imagine, according to his power that is at work within us, to him be glory in the church and in Christ Jesus throughout all generations, for ever and ever! Amen.[15]

> I can do everything through him who gives me strength.[16]

> Three times I pleaded with the Lord to take it [Paul's thorn in the flesh] away from me. But he said to me, "My grace is sufficient for you, for my power is made perfect in your weakness." Therefore I will boast all the more gladly about my weaknesses, so that Christ's power may rest on me. That is why, for Christ's sake, I delight in weaknesses, in insults, in hardships, in persecutions, in difficulties. For when I am weak, then I am strong.[17]

At my first defense, no one came to my support, but everyone deserted me. May it not be held against them. But the Lord stood at my side and gave me strength, so that the message might be fully proclaimed and all the Gentiles might hear it. And I was delivered from the lion's mouth. The Lord will rescue me from every evil attack and will bring me safely to his heavenly kingdom. To him be glory for ever and ever. Amen.[18]

11

Maturing through Confrontation

Receiving Rebuke When You Want to Return Fire

I was a senior in high school and had been attending the same church, with my parents, for five years. Too cool to ride the church bus to the youth devotional at a local park one Sunday evening, I came in my hot rod Chevelle. In my mind, I was the B.M.A.C. (Big Man at Church). I sat in the circle of the youth group, scoping out the chicks and acting religious when appropriate.

When the singing was over, the youth minister of the church, a guy named Ron, started sharing a Bible message. He asked a question, and I answered it. It's cool to act religious in these church settings, and it looks good to the religious girls. But on this night, I was in for the confrontation of my life.

153

Ron looked straight at me and asked, "What would you know about anything spiritual?"

We were all shocked. For a moment I thought I hadn't heard him correctly. No one in church had ever been that bold. My face turned red, and my whole body felt hot. I was embarrassed, and my little group of buddies were silently supporting me with their dropped heads and silent treatment of Ron.

Steadfastly he continued. Not too much later he asked another question. In an effort to regain some control and reestablish my position of pride, I began to answer.

But before I could, Ron interrupted and said, "I really don't want to hear from you. You have no part in this ministry, and you are not spiritually minded."

> Ron looked straight at me and asked, "What would you know about anything spiritual?"

Now, I was mad. I had been called to the carpet in front of my friends, and I was not going to bend or bow. *This means war*, I thought.

As soon as he broke the circle with a prayer and headed for the bus, a group of my buddies gathered around and began to hurl muffled, yet intentionally audible insults and complaints. As I made my way to my car, Ron intercepted me alone in an open area of the park. I thought momentarily, *Okay, he has come to his senses and realizes how wrong he was for treating me this way,* and I geared up for his apology.

Instead, he launched an exquisitely aimed volley of spiritual missiles into my camp. He opened by saying, "I love you, but I take nothing back that I said. It is all true. You are *not* spiritual, and you *are* immoral. Your life makes me feel like vomiting every time I think about it. It just makes me sick. I want you to stay away from the guys and the girls in our church until you repent. In fact, until you are willing to make some changes, you are not welcome at our youth gatherings." His eyes filled with tears as he walked onto the church bus.

In a storm of emotion, I squealed out of the parking lot, *Who does he think he is to talk to me that way? Hypocrite! What a jerk! If that's what church is all about, I don't want any part of it!* I thought as I pounded angrily on the steering wheel.

The following Wednesday, I called Ron from work. It was noon, and I thought the three days would probably be enough time for him to realize he couldn't do without me. He would see that he had made a big mistake, and besides, the Bible says you're not supposed to judge. (How handy that overused and misunderstood passage is when taken out of context.)

He answered the phone, and I tentatively, yet cheerfully, greeted him, "Hey Ron, this is Don. How's it goin'?" There was a pause.

"Have you decided to change your life?" he asked.

"Well, I don't quite see things the way you . . ."

He interrupted, "Why did you even call. You have ruined my lunch."

That was it. I slammed the phone down so hard it cracked the plastic casing. *I'm gonna tell my parents on this guy and they can tell the elders of the church. No youth minister should treat his poor helpless youth this way. We need to be encouraged for all we have to go through. This is spiritual abuse! When he sees that I mean business and that he might lose his cushy job, he'll think again before he goes rebuking someone publicly or privately.*

> Instead of running to the shepherds of our church to defend me, they knelt in fervent prayer that Ron would be filled with a spirit of courage and power to rebuke me.

My parents just didn't understand. What did I expect or even hope for? Instead of running to the shepherds of our church to defend their poor little baby, they knelt in fervent prayer that Ron would be filled with a spirit of courage and power. Some good it did to tell on him; they just sided with him. I remember thinking, *I can't wait to get out of this stupid house and away from this even more stupid church!*

Saturday of that same week was Ron's wedding. Both he and his fiancée were longtime friends, so I was expected to attend. I planned to slip through the receiving line undetected, give her a hug, and blow right past him. But just as I was slinking by, his right hand grasped mine, and his left caught hold of the back of my head. He pulled me right up tight and said, "When are you going to change your life?"

This guy was Robo-Preacher. I couldn't get him to stop his relentless commitment to getting me right with God, even if it meant hand-to-hand spiritual confrontation. His faith in God and God's ways led him to confront me in my sin, no matter what appeared to be at stake: our friendship, the attitudes of the rest of the youth group, the support of the youth's parents, or even his job.

So many possible excuses, yet he exercised none of them. I believe it was his willingness to confront that opened me up to be persuaded by God to turn my life around.

Confrontation Is Necessary

If you've read this section of the book in sequence, you'll have noticed that we are marking stages of maturity through some mountaintop experiences of God's people. We've already discussed two key mountains in the Israelite's history: Sinai, where they learned commitment, and Moriah, where they learned how to face testing. And now, to understand how heaven uses confrontation to mature us, let's go with Elijah and the Israelites and scale Mount Carmel, the mount of confrontation.[1]

You might be wondering why anyone would need a mountain of confrontation since God's covenant was secure and since his provisions are literally all around us. But the Israelites were like me, or I was like them: covenant and provision did not insure faithfulness and discipleship.

Remember, these are the people who made the golden "god groom" in the middle of their spiritual wedding ceremony.

When our story begins, one of the most wicked—if not *the* most wicked—ruling couples in the history of mankind was on the throne in Israel—Ahab and Jezebel. Through their misguidance, the nation of Israel had given up their Creator and Savior and were brazenly worshiping idols and committing acts of immorality in pagan rites of worship. Where would you begin to confront this mess? Where do we begin to confront the sin and immaturity in our own lives?

Elijah began by confronting himself.

If you were a young graduate of Jerusalem University with a major in Prophetic Ministry, you wouldn't have requested Israel as your first mission. But Elijah was called by God to go and confront the entire nation—from the top down, and from the bottom up. Let's pick up on the narrative in 1 Kings 18:

> Elijah said, "As the Lord Almighty lives, whom I serve, I will surely present myself to Ahab today."
>
> So Obadiah [devout believer and the man in charge of Ahab's palace] went to meet Ahab and told him, and Ahab went to meet Elijah. When he saw Elijah, he said to him, "Is that you, you troubler of Israel?"
>
> "I have not made trouble for Israel," Elijah replied. "But you and you father's family have. You have abandoned the Lord's commands and have followed the Baals."[2]

Jezebel was literally killing off the prophets who served Jehovah, and she and Ahab had searched the world over to put God's servant Elijah in the grave as well. The first person Elijah needed to confront was himself. He could not hope to persuade the rest of Israel to return to the dangerous business of following the Lord God, if he were wavering in his own convictions.

Elijah confronted the faithful.

Elijah's fellow disciple, Obadiah, was a devout believer who had even taken some risks up to this point, but he was in the king's employ and had learned to work within the system. His fear of Ahab was becoming stronger than his faith. But with a gentle confrontation from Elijah, Obadiah's courage and confidence got the boost he needed to begin taking risks again.

Unlike Elijah, we often give each other "spiritual professional courtesy" and let things go in each other's lives that actually are not acceptable to God. We can offer a myriad of excuses for not "sharpening each other"[3] or "spurring each other on to love and good deeds."[4] But prophets do not have the option of testing the spiritual winds of their listeners before they let the

> We often give each other "spiritual professional courtesy" and let things go in each other's lives that actually are not acceptable to God.

message of God blow through them. Even the faithful must at times be confronted.

Elijah openly confronted evil doers.

Once the *brethren* had been confronted, Elijah set a direct course for a head-on collision with Ahab. But Ahab was entrenched in sin and was not touched by Elijah's personal faith testimony nor his gentle confrontation. Instead, Ahab attempted to intimidate Elijah with false accusations and criticism. The prophet was unmoved and, in fact, went on the offense as he immediately reversed the indictment back to Ahab, the true troubler of Israel. God used Elijah to confront evil doers.

In verse 19 (of 1 Kings 18), Elijah assumed control of the confrontation and commanded Ahab, the king, to summon Israel to meet him on Mount Carmel. Then he took the offensive when he told Ahab, "Bring the four hundred and fifty prophets of Baal and the four hundred prophets of Asherah who eat at Jezebel's table."

His plan was to make sure *everyone* would know that there was a God in Israel and that this God had more power than Jezebel and all the false prophets she could round up. This was to be no secret battle over an insignificant enemy. He wasn't interested in fighting spiritual mini-wars. He was going for a full-blown, unmistakable victory over the forces of evil.

Our "confrontations" in the Body of Christ—as well as in the arenas of government, schools, and communities—are often little more than discussions among those who agree with us and perhaps with a few select outsiders whom we think we can control. The appearance of victory is often prize enough. The preservation or restoration of our own preferences is frequently our goal, instead of intense and total submission to the will of God. Not so with Elijah or his God!

God fiercely confronts any and all double-mindedness in us, and he expects us to confront it in each other.

Heavenly Confrontation

What are the identifying marks of heaven's confrontation, and what response do they require?

When Israel, Ahab, and the false prophets appeared on the mountain, Elijah immediately took the lead again and issued a direct confrontation to them all. Elijah went before the people and said, "How long will you waver between two opinions? If the Lord is God, follow him; but if Baal is God, follow him."

Heavenly confrontation makes the choices clear.

Subtleties are out; speaking the truth is in. Jesus himself said that you cannot serve two masters, that you cannot put your hand to the plow and turn back, and that you're either for him or against him.[5] Confrontation is about choices.

It is interesting to note that Elijah employs an ironic word play in verse 21 that is related to the pagan worship of verse 26. The Hebrew word for "waver" in verse 21 is the same as that used for "danced" in verse 26. The people were trying to have enough of God the Creator to secure his blessings, while maintaining their evil and immoral Baal worship. Elijah called this "dancing" between two opinions.

But Elijah drew a line in the sand and demanded that a choice be made. He set the stage and explained the rules of the contest: Two lords. Two teachings. Two lifestyles. Two sets of followers. Two bulls. Two altars. Two pleas for fire. The choices were clearly before them. They could not have it both ways.

Many Christians I know are doing the *double-life two-step* of the ancient Israelites, and God will confront them to persuade them to choose him alone. It was God who put this mountain before ancient Israel through Elijah and before me as a teenager through Ron. And considering the spiritual condition of America, I anticipate we are all in for a long climb on Mount Confrontation.

> The people were trying to have enough of God the Creator to secure his blessings, while maintaining their evil and immoral Baal worship. Elijah called this "dancing" between two opionions.

Heavenly confrontation expects resistance.

One of the most difficult confrontations came at the end of verse 21: "But the people said nothing." You don't have to live long or confront often before you face the silent treatment. Silence does not mean agreement, and in this case, it might even represent anger and a desire to get revenge on this loud, obnoxious holy man.

When was the last time someone really rebuked you? How did you deal with it? Were you like me with Ron—angry, but hoping your friend would get over it and just let it drop? Heavenly confrontation is often resisted, but if we want to benefit from its message of hope and relationship, we will bow our knee to the Lord and accept his confrontation.

Heavenly confrontation exposes evil.

It was time for a showdown, and Elijah let the prophets of Baal go first. "They called on the name of Baal from morning till noon. 'O Baal, answer us!' they shouted. But there was no response; no one answered. And they danced around the altar they had made."[6]

Then Elijah, whose confidence was growing, laid the groundwork for their complete defeat with a touch of sacred sarcasm.

> At noon Elijah began to taunt them. "Shout louder!" he said. "Surely he is a god! Perhaps he is deep in thought, or busy, or traveling. Maybe he is sleeping and must be awakened." So they shouted louder and slashed themselves with swords and spears, as was their custom, until their blood flowed. Midday passed, and they continued their frantic prophesying until the time for the evening sacrifice. But there was no response, no one answered, no one paid attention.[7]

Confrontation is tough on false gods.

Notice that when their first attempt to win with a losing god brought absolutely no response, they simply put more time, effort, and energy into the same losing strategy. They were so desperate that they even allowed the opposing team to coach them.

Many of us, too, have chosen approaches to life that appeal to us, but don't yield the results we hope for. Early failures and poor returns force us to inflate and exaggerate our reports of success, yet we privately recognize that something is amiss. My "cool" exterior in high school was a shallow cover for a lifestyle that *really didn't work*. Ron was right. I was wrong. And I knew it even better than he did.

> Our addiction to the appearance of personal success is part of what makes confrontation so hard to receive.

It's pretty difficult to defend your side of a debate when all you have is surface pride and the appearance of success, but very few of us want to admit to any misstep, miscue, or that anything is missing. This addiction to the appearance of personal success is part of what makes confrontation so hard to receive. Like the prophets of Baal, we surround ourselves with a mutual admiration society, and we avoid anyone who suggests that our "emperor has no clothes." We recycle and rename the same old losing game plans, but expect different results. How foolish!

Just as Elijah exposed the evil in his day, there is much in our time that needs exposing. Our national understanding of what it means to be a Christian has suffered greatly. Many are so converted to their churches and their cultural versions of Christianity that the words of Jesus himself have little impact. Racial prejudice, mean-spirited conversation, grudgeful hearts, and a lack of generosity often go unchallenged. Some even go out of their ways to avoid contact with orphans and widows, in spite of the fact that the Bible defines caring for orphans and widows as "pure religion." Too often, we fail to confront the issues that matter most because we're already emotionally spent from challenging the issues on our narrow list of "pet sins"—issues that are rarely of eternal significance and that rarely demand personal change.

Living in Christ means just that: living as Christ would live. When heaven confronts the evil in our lives, may our hearts be open.

Heavenly confrontation expects persecution.

Because he confronted the Baal worshipers, Elijah was accused of being the one who was causing all the trouble for Israel. But in actuality, it wasn't even Elijah who was doing the confronting—it was God. Heaven hoped, through the emotional upheaval of the Mount Carmel confrontation, that an opening could be found in the hearts of God's people to persuade them to return to him.

Many great people have been severely criticized as troublemakers because they see things from a different point of view *and* are willing to verbalize their concerns. As early as 1932, Winston Churchill tried to rouse his nation and the world to the danger of Nazi Germany. The buildup of the German armed forces alarmed him, and he pleaded for a powerful British air force.

But he was called a warmonger. His message was not popular, and he was criticized for it. Of course, he was no longer called a warmonger after September 1, 1939, when the Nazi forces invaded and overran Europe, beginning World War II.

God confronts to save lives, both presently and eternally. Many families, churches, communities, and countries could become life-giving, if they could be persuaded to listen to, and live by, the voice of God. But it takes prophets like Elijah, who count the pain of the contest worth the salvation of the lost, to bring about real change.

Heavenly confrontation involves everyone who will participate.

After hours of shouting and dancing and prophesying, it was finally evident that Baal was not God. Now it was time for the true God to show his power. But Elijah did not hoard all the victory.

I appreciate what he said to all the people. He said, *"Come here to me."* Elijah was committed to making this *a victory for everyone* who wanted to serve the Lord. This must always be central to any confrontation.

Elijah brought the people up close, and rebuilt the altar of the Lord with twelve stones—one for each of the twelve tribes of Israel. The significance of this may elude us, but it would not escape the attention of a nation that had been bitterly divided—North and South—for nearly eighty years. A twelve-stone altar in the ten-tribe North made a statement of spiritual solidarity for all to see.

And then, Elijah gave the people the chance to participate in the victory by involving them in preparing the altar for the fire from heaven. He had them pour water over the entire altar and sacrifice three times. Perhaps, without the people even realizing it, they had joined the team of the One doing the confronting.

Heavenly confrontation does not give up until God has been exalted.

Elijah's prayer in 1 Kings 18:36 made it clear that God was really the leader of that confrontation:

> At the time of sacrifice, the prophet Elijah stepped forward and prayed: "O Lord, God of Abraham, Isaac, and Israel, let it be known today that you are God in Israel and that I am your servant and have done all these things at your command."

Elijah didn't even get out the "Amen" before fire descended from the Lord and burned up everything that was even close to that water-logged sacrifice! (Talk about heaven in the real world!) Now it was evident to all that there was one God, one covenant, one proclamation, one commitment, one lifestyle, and one group of followers. God was exalted.

When all the people saw this, they fell prostrate and cried, "The Lord—he is God! The Lord—he is God!"[8]

Heavenly confrontation bears fruit for God.

Elijah's prayer in verse 37 announced exactly what God was doing on the Mountain of Confrontation: "Answer me, O Lord, answer me, so these people will know that you, O Lord, are God, and that you are turning their hearts back again."[9] God's intent was to bear fruit for heaven—and the people were persuaded. They turned back to the God who had married them at Sinai and had revealed himself as the Almighty Provider to Abraham on Moriah. God had won them back, but not without confrontation.

When our hearts are open to the Lord, confrontation doesn't take all morning, afternoon, and evening or a bunch of frantic religious activity. God bears fruit when we accept and mature from his confrontation.

Heaven Confronts Us for Our Good

God does not put the Mountain of Confrontation in our lives to torment us. He confronts to save. We are in a serious battle with Satan, and God knows that when we stray from his path, we fall into Satan's pit.

> No discipline seems pleasant at the time, but painful. Later on, however, it produces a harvest of righteousness and peace for those who have been trained by it.[10]

> Our struggle is not against flesh and blood, but against the rulers, against the authorities, against the

powers of this dark world and against the spiritual forces of evil in the heavenly realms.[11]

For although we live in this world, we do not wage war as the world does. The weapons we fight with are not the weapons of the world. On the contrary, they have divine power to demolish strongholds. We demolish arguments and every pretension that sets itself up against the knowledge of God, and we take captive every thought to make it obedient to Christ.[12]

When we are judged by the Lord, we are being disciplined so that we will not be condemned with the world.[13]

And God confronts us because he knows how easily we can be deceived. The human conscience can be seared. Our minds can be darkened by foolish reasoning, and our emotions can be hardened toward the Lord and his wisdom. Thinking, feeling, and making decisions by the mere appearance of things often lead to false judgments of God, man, and what we should be doing with our lives. Were it not for the courage of Ron, I would not have faced the truth about my life and have been persuaded to surrender to God.

Confrontation is a method God uses in our lives, exactly when and where we need it. We must diligently direct our souls to the purpose of confrontation so that our minds and hearts will remain open to the potential growth that comes as a result.

12 Maturing through Serving

Reaching Out When You Feel Like Reeling In

A fine Christian lady showed up at my office for her "appointment with the minister." She was neatly dressed and courteous. After a somewhat terse greeting, she took a seat and maintained an erect posture. Pulling some notes from her Bible, she began to read for me her carefully scripted resignation from teaching Sunday school at this church ever again. In all her thirty years of faithful service, she had been passed over and overlooked one too many times. There was no gratitude for this thankless job, she said, " . . . not that I ever expected any."

As she wound down her resignation/here's-what-I-really-think-of-you-ungrateful-people note, she made a

171

statement that altered my life. Here it is: "I don't mind serving, but I will not tolerate being treated like a servant."

Wow! Although she certainly didn't intend for me to take her statement the way I did, I will be forever impacted by it. In fact, her statement is what lies at the heart of the lethargy and ineffectiveness of the church today. People want to serve, but they flatly refuse to take on the identity of a servant.

> The crowning act of maturity comes in the voluntary removal of the crown.

What's the big difference? A person can choose to serve from any station in life. The CEO of a company may strap on an apron once a year to serve his employees a chicken dinner at the company picnic, but no one is confused on Monday morning as to who's in charge. Former President Bush remarked, "It's amazing how many people can beat you at golf once you are no longer president." Service changes your behavior, not your identity.

But becoming a servant is nothing less than embracing an identity. It is accepting a position in which humility *is your only recourse.* Servants serve as an extension of who they are. Perhaps the crowning act of maturity comes in the voluntary removal of the crown.

The ancient Christ-hymn shared in Philippians 2 states where Jesus was in this regard: "Your attitude should be the same as that of Christ Jesus: Who, being in very nature God, did not consider equality with God something to be grasped, but made himself nothing, taking the very nature of a servant, being made in human likeness."[1]

When heaven came to the real world, the Sovereign changed his identity and came as a servant. In our self-absorbed society where getting, flaunting, and hoarding seem to be the measure of it all, the concept of servanthood is nearly anathema. Even in the church, as evidenced by the lady mentioned earlier, being a servant is out of the question.

In his poignant book, *Descending into Greatness*, author Bill Hybels makes the following observation:

> One way to track the pulse of a society is to measure its words. Their meanings and values change with the times and movements of history. Take the word "servant." Before complaint became a national way of life, it was considered an honor to serve someone. There was no higher cause than to provide for the needs of others out of love. Yet in a culture that panders to self-expression and individualism, "servant" has virtually disappeared from our vocabularies. The six o'clock news features one self-absorbed person after another demanding his or her individual rights. Occasionally a newscast ends with a "human-interest" story on someone who serves others. What surprises us is not that this person is featured, but the obvious fact that the servant—one who looks after more than his own self-interest—is now considered a novelty, the odd man out.[2]

All this self-advancement and glorification has left us in an infantile state emotionally and relationally. One forty-year-old professional confessed during a counseling session,

"I've acted like a twelve-year-old most of my life. Not a bad job if you can get away with it. I basically did what I wanted when I wanted. I only realized how destructive this was when, after three kids and fourteen anniversaries, my wife told me I was barely above repulsive and she no longer had any feelings for me."

Service for the sake of personal advancement is more nauseating than blatant selfishness. Again Hybels observes, "From the world's perspective, [up] is the only direction to go. Do whatever it takes to conquer gravity. Whether you do it blatantly or wear the disguise of humility, make yourself upwardly mobile."

However, when heaven descended into our world, it wore no disguise. Jesus came fully dressed as a servant, inside and out. And he calls us to the same. How can we let go of the world's trappings of service and brazenly take on the nature of a servant?

The key to servanthood is illustrated powerfully in the lives of Moses and Christ. No matter what they did or where they went, they were secure in the presence of God. Jesus could wash feet, according to John 13:3–5, because he knew he came from God and was going back to God. He had total assurance of his relationship with God. Jesus did not need the accolades of the world because he was carried by the applause of heaven.

But what about Moses? He was someone like us who had only experienced heaven from this side. How did he mature beyond service to being a servant, the most humble man in all the earth?

Fifteen centuries before Christ, God called Moses from his comfortable job of taking care of his father-in-law's sheep to the role of leading a million-plus people from the cruel oppression of the most powerful country on earth to the Promised Land. In God's great wisdom he had been maturing Moses for eighty years to prepare him for this next great step: he was commissioned into the ministry of God.

At three months of age, Moses was found in his floating hideaway by the daughter of the king of Egypt, who adopted him into her family and renamed him Moses. Under the watchful eye of God through Moses' older sister, Miriam, his own mother was hired as a nanny and paid to nurse and nurture her son in the palace of the oppressing king. He was educated in all the wisdom of the Egyptians and became powerful in speech and action. The future deliverer was being taught and trained by the very oppressors he would overthrow.

According to the first Christian martyr, Moses was forty years old when he first sensed an awareness of who he was and what he should do.

> When Moses was forty years old, he decided to visit his fellow Israelites. He saw one of them being mistreated by an Egyptian, so he went to his defense and avenged him by killing the Egyptian. Moses thought that his own people would realize that God was using him to rescue them, but they did not.[3]

Take a good look at that! Moses had something in his heart to do, but it was not the right time. When he put himself on the line, his own people took offense at him and even criticized him.

> The next day, Moses came upon two Israelites who were fighting. He tried to reconcile them by saying, "Men, you are brothers; why do you want to hurt each other?" But the man who was mistreating the other pushed Moses and said, "Who made you ruler and judge over us? Do you want to kill me as you killed the Egyptian yesterday?"[4]

Things went from bad to worse. Not only did his own people not see him as a rescuer, they were caustic and pushy. Whether they thought he was Egyptian royalty, or worse yet, a favored Hebrew who had avoided the plight of his suffering brethren, they had no use for him. They would not have even flinched if he were caught and executed for his heroic act of saving the Israelite.

How would you respond? It's tough to put yourself on the line for something you believe in when outward opposition is fierce, but it's even worse when the rejection and resistance come from within. When people fighting on the same side wound or kill each other, the military calls it "friendly fire." It's an odd name for such a terrible activity, yet it accurately represents the shock and shame of discovering that your dead and wounded bear the identifying marks of your own artillery. To be treated poorly by the enemy is expected, but when we are hunted and hurt by our own, the scars are much deeper—in part, because we are so vulnerable to them.

Moses' response is quite natural and expected; yet, as we will see, it was just the next step in his development toward becoming the deliverer of Israel. "Then Moses was afraid and thought, 'What I did must have become known.' When Pharaoh heard of this, he tried to kill Moses, but Moses fled from Pharaoh and went to live in Midian."[5]

Maturing through service means that your first work may not be your greatest work.

While living in Midian for forty years, he married into the family of Jethro, priest of Midian. This man was powerful, wise, and wealthy. While Moses was in Midian, God was able to work several key parts of the plan to deliver his people from Egypt. First, the Pharaoh, who put the price on Moses' head, died. Next, Moses became an expert in the terrain of the Sinai Peninsula, where he would some-day lead the people of Israel. And

Maturing through service means that your first work may not be your greatest.

finally, the people of Israel were growing tired of their ago-nizing predicament and would be much more open to a deliverer.

Meanwhile, Moses was totally oblivious to God's plan and was comfortable in his rural life. He had married and raised a family, he had a good relationship with the in-laws, and he was *eighty years old*. (Most of us would be thinking about retirement at that age—Fort Myers in a Winnebago or bust!) Who would even imagine that his greatest commis-sion in life was yet to come?

In the middle of all this, heaven descended to Mount Horeb. Follow along in Exodus chapter 3: "Now Moses was tending the flock of Jethro his father-in-law, the priest of Midian, and he led the flock to the far side of the desert and came to Horeb, the mountain of God."[6]

Moses' entire life was about to be tossed into total confusion and then totally explained *in the same commission.*

> There the angel of the Lord appeared to him in flames of fire from within a bush. Moses saw that though the bush was on fire it did not burn up. So Moses thought, "I will go over and see this strange sight—why the bush does not burn up." When the Lord saw that he had gone over to look, God called to him from within the bush, "Moses! Moses!" And Moses said, "Here I am."[7]

Now I don't know for sure why God said his name twice, unless Moses passed out on the first call, and was awakened by the second. I am always amazed at Bible characters' responses to situations like this. When bushes, donkeys, or anything else talked to them, they just answered like one of us picking up the phone!

> Then God said, "Do not come any closer." [Now that's one command that would not have been necessary if I had been on that mountain.] "Take off your sandals, for the place where you are standing is holy ground. I am the God of Abraham, the God of Isaac, and the God of Jacob." The introduction was overwhelming, and Moses hid himself in fear. The Lord said, "I have seen the misery of my people in Egypt. I have heard

them crying out because of their slave drivers, and I am concerned about their suffering. So I have come down to rescue them . . . and bring them up out of that land into a good and spacious land, a land flowing with milk and honey."[8]

Moses was an Israelite. This was precious news to him. Heaven had not forgotten about the real world. God was coming down to rescue his people! Moses still had a sister and brother in Egypt as well as other friends and relatives he'd left behind. The pains of the Israelites had stirred Moses' heart four decades earlier, and now God was finally going to help them. Amen! That's great! Praise the Lord! I'll be thinking about you while you're on your way. Send a pyramid postcard, if your think about it.

Then God said to Moses, "So now, go. I am sending *you* to Pharaoh to bring my people the Israelites out of Egypt."[9]

"What?" The conversation had been going great up to that point. God had waxed eloquent about his concerns for Israel and his plans to finally make good on the covenant he had made with their forefathers, but what is this business of dragging Moses into the plan? Moses' first words in reply were, "Who am I, that I should go to Pharaoh and bring the Israelites out of Egypt?"[10]

Moses was about to learn the first lesson of Mount Horeb: *Maturing through service means I become the servant.* Everyone loves a commission. It's exciting to think of embarking on some great mission that captivates the imagination of the explorer buried deep within all of us. But the extent of our involvement is watching the coverage on CNN. We want someone to do it, but we are content to take a spectator position.

Think through history. Columbus got some support and a good send off by a king and queen who never set foot on one of his ships. Charles Lindbergh was cheered mostly by those who stayed firmly on the ground. The McDonald brothers (think Golden Arches) were content to let Ray Kroc take all the risks to make them rich. Missionaries are often deeply respected for their commitment, but from a very comfortable distance. I have personally made the observation that everyone wants to be inspired by Helen Keller and Christopher Reeves, but no one wants to *be* them.

Through the next several verses in Exodus 3 and 4, Moses fired questions and excuses at God like a machine gun, hoping to shoot down this idea.

- Who am I?[11]

- Suppose I go to the Israelites and say to them, "The God of your fathers has sent me to you," and they ask me, "What is his name?" Then what shall I tell them?[12]

- What if they do not believe me or listen to me and say, "The Lord did not appear to you"? [This is reminiscent of the reaction he got forty years earlier when he ended up fleeing Egypt in the first place.][13]

- O Lord, I have never been eloquent, neither in the past nor since you have spoken to your servant. I am slow of speech and tongue. [Moses is saying, "God, I've never been the kind of guy you're lookin' for, and our little meeting hasn't changed things."][14]

- Then Moses finally said, "O Lord [can't you just hear the weary whimper in his voice as he goes for one last ditch effort to dissuade God from this foolishness?], *please send someone else to do it.*"[15]

That was the bottom line all along, as it is with us. When we realize how much we are actually going to have to give up to become a servant, we are unnerved. Many refuse to become true servants because they will not exercise the faith it takes to trust God for what we used to get through our own prideful accomplishments.

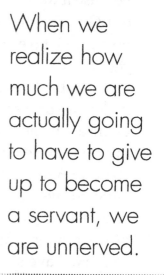

When we realize how much we are actually going to have to give up to become a servant, we are unnerved.

Any one of the excuses he gave would have been enough for Moses— if God would only let him off the hook. But the God of commission is persistent. Moses had been in preparation under the tutelage of God himself. The time had come to step up and take his place in God's great plan to bring healing and freedom to the oppressed. Stephen reminds us, according to Luke, "This is the same Moses whom they had rejected with the words, 'Who made you ruler and judge?' He was sent to be their ruler and deliverer by God himself."[16]

God was the commissioner, but forty years of internal and external influences on Moses' life had cooled his passion and cost him his sense of mission for the deliverance of Israel. The statements of others and his own view of himself had become mountains in themselves that had to be moved by God. To fulfill God's calling, Moses had to change. He had to mature and become something more than he was at the time of the call.

Now Moses was about to learn the second lesson of Mount Horeb: *Maturing through service means serving where God leads.* There was much more to this mountaintop experience than God's leading forward and Moses' holding back, because it didn't end in a stalemate. Moses did go! Just what did God say and do that convinced Moses to step it up a notch and take on this calling? God said, *"I will be with you."*[17]

With statements of encouragement, miracles, and patient assurance, God revealed the most profound element of life available to every one of us: *God is with us.* The power to move Moses from a life of private predictability to the chaos of fighting for the restoration of freedom and hope to battered lives came from the simple promise of God's presence. If God was going with Moses, then not a single excuse or reservation was valid.

We have spent too much time in our generation picking at what is wrong with us instead of praising what is right with God! If God is for us, who can be against us?[18] He will never leave us or forsake us.[19] He will be with us always, even to the end of the age.[20] The presence of the Lord was the power that lifted all the great lives of God's followers into the league of history-makers.

Elijah, the greatest prophet of the Old Testament, faced this same struggle seven centuries later on the exact same mountain. Following God's awesome display of power and presence in the Mount Carmel dual, he was scared to death, and out of town, by Queen Jezebel. He ran out into the wilderness and prayed for death to take him. He said to God, "I've had enough, Lord. Take my life; I am no better than any of my ancestors."[21]

Why the deep depression? Why the loss of passion and mission? The problem was clearly revealed when Elijah got to Mount Horeb: "And the word of the Lord came to him: 'What are you doing here, Elijah?'"

His answer is so enlightening: "He replied, 'I have been very zealous for the Lord God Almighty. The Israelites have rejected your covenant, broken down your altars, and put your prophets to death with the sword. *I* am the only one left, and now they are trying to kill me too.'"[22]

The "I"s have it. Where was *God* in the work of Elijah? Was it not God who returned the hearts of his people to himself on Mount Carmel? Yes, but I have been in Elijah's frame of mind more times than I care to divulge. How would God get Elijah back on track and reconnected to the commission?

The Lord said, "Go out and stand on the mountain in the *presence* of the Lord, for the Lord is about to pass by."[23]

In showing himself to Elijah, God revealed three essential certainties about his presence in our lives. *First, God is present even when we do not feel it.* When fear and depression dull our senses and darken our souls, God is still present and willing to give us what we need for our journey.

Second, God is not bound to show up as we expect, because he is God. We often want him to blow into a situation *(the wind)*, shake it up *(the earthquake)*, and burn, or at least singe *(the fire)*, people we perceive as the root of our problems. Instead, God comes in a gentle whisper to our souls and says, "What are you doing here?"[24] In effect: I am your God, and I've shared with you through my mirror what to do with your life. How did you get off over here in the wastelands of pride, anger, revenge, jealously, backbiting, and accusations?

Finally, God reminds us once again that he is in control. Elijah complained that he was the only real faithful follower of God, but that was based on Elijah's myopic, pious comparisons. Elijah didn't know what he was talking about. God flatly declared, "Yet I have seven thousand in Israel—all whose knees have not bowed down to Baal and all whose mouths have not kissed him."[25]

You think Elijah might be feeling a little sheepish at this moment? Living in the presence of God is radically life changing. Moses and Elijah met with God on the Mountain of Service, and he commissioned them to be his servants. But notice that God is not a commander who commissions his troops from the rear. They felt his presence and absorbed it into their personal lives. The presence of God gave them the confidence to accept and live the commission they were given.

When Jesus himself went to the Mount of Transfiguration, Luke described it this way:

> About eight days after Jesus said this, he took Peter,
> John, and James with him and went up onto a moun-
> tain to pray. As he was praying, the appearance of his
> face changed, and his clothes became as bright as a
> flash of lightening. Two men, Moses and Elijah,
> appeared in glorious splendor, talking with Jesus.
> They spoke about his departure, which he was about
> to bring to fulfillment at Jerusalem.[26]

They spoke with him about his departure . . . that he
was about to bring to fulfillment at Jerusalem. What was
this about? It was about the mission Jesus came to fulfill—
his suffering and crucifixion. He was determined to remain
firmly planted in the presence of the Father so that he could
serve the purpose for which he came to earth.

At this point, I think it is obvious why two experienced
mountaineers like Moses and Elijah were sent to share with
Jesus in this particular discussion. They knew the tremen-
dous temptation to back out on the work of God. They
understood, and had even verbalized, every possible excuse
for getting out while the getting was good. But their message to Jesus was one of strength and power, for they also
knew the reviving strength of God's presence. They saw
armies fall, water come from rocks, bread and meat drop
from the sky, the dead raised, the rain stop and start at their
word, the Red Sea part, and lunch delivered by ravens.

God told the entire nation of Israel when they were
camped at Mount Horeb, "You have stayed long enough at
this mountain. Break camp and advance."[27]

I believe it's time to ring this message through every
home, church, community, and government office in the

land. We have been here long enough. God has promised his presence among us, and thus has blessed us with everything we will ever need to do any great work in his name. But now it's time to take on the identity of *servants*—servants of God, each other, and the lost.

Start a ministry. Call a neighbor. Drive a disabled person to the store or doctor. Smile at every kid and grown-up you see. Tip generously, no matter what the service—especially breakfast servers who have worked all night. Don't tailgate. Watch your language. Volunteer with kids. Visit the hospital and nursing home. Tutor struggling students. Say yes at a church business meeting. Pray.

Send a card. Let someone else go first at the four-way stop. Don't fret out loud in line behind the lady with four kids at the grocery store. Hold the door. Read Scripture and good books to children. Give back rubs and gentle hugs. Throw baseballs and lose graciously at Monopoly. Vote for children in the womb who can't look you in the eye yet. Make marriage fun. Encourage business owners. Work hard, but don't complain. Sponsor a poor child. Send anonymous gifts to missionaries. Listen to sweet widows who love the Lord. Plan to take care of people. Invent ways to make people happy.

You get the idea. Servanthood ever-expands the presence and transforming power of God in us, thus maturing us to more clearly reflect heaven in the real world.

> This is how we know what love is: Jesus Christ laid down his life for us. And we ought to lay down our lives for our brothers. If anyone has material posses-

sions and sees his brother in need but has no pity on him, how can the love of God be in him? Dear children, let us not love with words or tongue but with actions and in truth. This then is how we know that we belong to the truth, and how we set our hearts at rest in his presence. [28]

Maturity begins by confessing that your life is not what it should be, could be, or would be if you lived daily in the acute awareness of the presence of God.

Change the way you think and feel about the mountains God has been putting in your life. The *pain* you encounter through total commitment to God is light and temporary compared to the reward of living together with God for all eternity.

You will face many *tests on* Mount Moriah, for "we must go through many hardships to enter the kingdom of God."[29] But when you are called, follow. Get up, saddle your donkey, chop the wood, and head straight for the place God tells you to go. When you get there, don't let anything get in your way, and God will provide. Do this often enough, and you will get the hang of standing firm by faith.

He who begins this work in us will bring it to completion,[30] and that means *confrontation* on Mount Carmel. We need to accept, and even request, the discipline of the Lord. We do not ever need to be afraid of the Lord's honest exposure of our weaknesses and sin, because we are secure in his circle of love. His discipline is a way of showing love. Even when all we feel is his soul-bruising chastening, in faith we know we are being spared a crushing blow from Satan, designed to knock us out of our spiritual refuge.

Enough time has been wasted on pride; it's time to learn *servanthood* on Mount Horeb. It's long past time for Christians to get hot about Satan's work in the world. Every victory he scores costs heaven another soul. Time has come for the forceful advancement of the kingdom through us as individuals involved in hand-to-hand spiritual combat with the forces of darkness.

> "In the final choice, a soldier's pack is not so heavy a burden as a prisoner's chains."

Our fears do not control us or keep us from pushing the lines of Satan back and rescuing the captives. As Dwight Eisenhower once said, "In the final choice, a soldier's pack is not so heavy a burden as a prisoner's chains." We who are empowered by the presence of the living God consider no weight too great to keep us from fulfilling our commission to lead people to Jesus, who *is* heaven in the real world. And in order to bring people to Jesus, we must come down from the mountain and enter the valley of life. Steven Curtis Chapman and Geoff Moore have written a beautiful song, "The Mountain," expressing this very idea.

> I want to build a house up on this mountain
> Way up high where the peaceful waters flow
> To quench my thirsty soul up on the mountain
> I can see for miles up on this mountain
> Troubles seem so small they almost disappear
> Lord, I love it here up on the mountain

My faith is strengthened by all that I see
You make it easy for me to believe up on the mountain
Oh, up on the mountain
I would love to live up on this mountain
And keep the pain of living life so far away
But I know I can't stay up on the mountain

I said I'd go, Lord, wherever You lead
For where You are is where I most want to be
And I can tell we're headed for the valley
My faith is strengthened by all that I've seen
So Lord help me remember what You've shown me
Up on the mountain

You bring me up here on the mountain
For me to rest and learn and grow
I see the truth up on the mountain
And I carry it to the world far below
So as I go down to the valley
Knowing that You will go with me
This is my prayer, Lord
Help me to remember what You've shown me
Up on the mountain
Up on the mountain

I cherish these times up on the mountain
But I can leave this place because I know
Someday You'll take me home to live forever
Up on the mountain[31]

Conclusion

God's Pledge of Allegiance

Heaven in the real world is the transforming power of God finding present-day expression in the lives of Christians just like you. It's the message of heaven taking firm root in our hearts and minds. It's the model of heaven captivating our desires, priorities, and behaviors. It's the method of heaven to bring maturity and stability to our reactions and relationships.

God has a method to his plan for our maturity. He knows exactly what we need, and he's patient enough to keep leading even when we are extremely immature in our response to him. Pain, testing, confrontation, and servanthood are the tools God uses to fashion us. Those who have been transformed by the careful workmanship of God become people of unbelievable power and influence.

191

Let us fix our eyes on Jesus, the author and perfecter of our faith, who for the joy set before him endured the cross, scorning its shame, and sat down at the right hand of the throne of God. Consider him who endured such opposition from sinful men, so that you will not grow weary and lose heart. . . . Endure hardship as discipline. . . . No discipline seems pleasant at the time, but painful. Later on, however, it produces a harvest of righteousness and peace for those who have been trained by it.[1]

Therefore, I urge you, brothers, in view of God's mercy, to offer your bodies as living sacrifices, holy and pleasing to God—this is your spiritual act of worship. Do not conform any longer to the pattern of this world, but be transformed by the renewing of your mind. Then you will be able to test and approve what God's will is—his good, pleasing, and perfect will.[2]

Since, then, you have been raised with Christ, set your hearts on things above . . . not on earthly things. For you died, and your life is now hidden with Christ in God. When Christ, who is your life, appears, then you also will appear with him in glory.[3]

I ask you to make a pledge to God—a pledge to devote your life to him as he has given his life for you, a pledge to accept his message, imitate his model, and to embrace his methods for maturing you.

How do we as humans identify true and lasting commitment? For most of us, our first actual statement of commitment (outside of telling our mommies we love them), is reciting the Pledge of Allegiance. Francis Bellamy's pledge of allegiance to the flag of the United States of America was first proclaimed by public school children in 1892 at the National School Celebration, marking the four hundredth anniversary of the discovery of America. It is a basic requirement for citizenship. But what does this pledge mean to us? Tracing the impact of the pledge on my life has helped me understand the process of recognizing and developing deeper commitments.

Do you recall the pledge in first grade? I remember my right hand properly resting over the upper left of my little chest, proudly taking my place with twenty-two other first graders in Miss Hartke's class to recite our national memory verse. Every day. Same stroke of the clock. Same stance. Same stare. Same statements. In grade school, the pledge was primarily verbal and mechanical.

Then when Mike, a teenager from our church, went to Vietnam, the pledge grew to take on a deeper meaning. It was as if the pledge was becoming a part of me. Our family lived patriotism, and the news of the war and concern for our uniformed countrymen was daily diet for nearly a decade. Scenes of flag-draped, standard-issue caskets carried by smartly dressed trustees of our freedom burned permanent images into my soul. My parents taught that this sacrifice was their pledge of allegiance to our country, and specifically to me. It became difficult to recite the pledge without tears threatening to burst the dams of my tightly closed eyes. No longer mechanical, the pledge had become emotional.

Then as an adult, I took my family to the Vietnam Veterans Memorial in Washington. Although only one of my many visits to the Wall, this was the first as a father longing to pass on the price of freedom to his children.

Huddled with my family at the "Granite Mirror," I stared at the reflection of their freedom, laced with the names of their silenced guardians. Over the still waters of the Reflecting Pool rose the harmony of a high school choir singing the National Anthem from the steps of Lincoln's Memorial. As if by the beat of a conductor's wand, our hands moved in unison to cover our hearts. Our eyes were fixed on a windswept American flag reflected in the black stone. Allegiance is not circumstantial. Sacrifice is not seasonal. Loyalty is a lifestyle. The pledge had become spiritual.

For God, his allegiance is more than verbal, and never mechanical. It even goes beyond emotion. In the act of creation, God pledged his allegiance to us. Simply being the author and producer of something makes you accountable. If the design fails, the designer is called into judgment.

God is God. He knew creating us in his image bore the potential for problems. Creating is itself an act of choice. Choice is central to his nature. And just as God had already experienced with Satan, giving people the power of choice meant giving up complete control over your own creation. Would his people choose him? Would they love him? Choice means he would choose not to dictate the outcome.

He created anyway. It was worth it to him. He is filled with love, and he lives to love. The thought of being friends with those who would turn to him outweighed the risk of being cursed, cut, and killed by those who would turn on him.

For God, nearness to your heart is not a matter of crisis or circumstance. Candidly, he can't get over you. He is the undaunted suitor of the divine romance. He is the lover who keeps writing, calling, and coming to see you—not for what he wants from you, but to share what he has pledged to you.

When you and I frustrate his efforts to show us his love, his passion only intensifies. We can never be more than one step away from him, because he constantly makes up the distance between us, except for the one step we must take toward him.

Heaven is in the real world because God made a spiritual pledge to you and me. Take a step closer to God with me right now. And all who have truly experienced the difference he makes in life will never live without him again. You may be skeptical, or even fearful, to add anyone or anything to the mix of your life, after all you've been through. The Lord knows that. So he is gentle, patient, and sensitive. He doesn't even mind your reading his love letter over and over to check out his resume and credentials. He has gone out of his way to offer himself to you and me through his model, Jesus Christ. And since we are already facing hardships, let's at least give him the opportunity to work those difficulties into our lives in positive ways.

Well, the book is done, and we both remain as eternal souls—souls with a destiny. Join me in giving God unlimited access to bring heaven into our real world.

Take a moment and read John 3:16–17 with me. Slow down. Imagine yourself raised like a flag onto a gleaming mast. Watch with wonder as God himself approaches, places his hand over his heart, and recites his pledge of allegiance to you:

> I so loved the world, that I gave my only begotten Son. That if you believe in him, you will not die, but will have eternal life. For I did not send my Son into the world to condemn you, but to save you.

Notes

Preface

1. Steven Curtis Chapman, "Heaven in the Real World" (Sparrow Song/Peach Hill Songs Admin. by EMI Christian Music Publishing, 1994).

Introduction

1. Isa. 40:26.
2. Phil. 3:14.

PART ONE
Accepting Heaven's Message:
Newness through Relationship

Prelude

1. John 5:37.
2. Rom. 10:17.

Chapter One
Heaven's Priority: Restoring Your Value

1. 2 Pet. 3:9.
2. Matt. 13:44.

3. Deut. 4:7.
4. James 4:8.
5. Phil. 3:20.
6. Deut. 26:18.
7. Steven Curtis Chapman and Geoff Moore, "Treasure of You" (Sparrow Song/Peach Hill Songs, Starstruck Music Admin. by EMI Christian Music Publishers, 1994).

Chapter Two
Heaven's Provision: Offering Total Pardon

1. Matt. 18:21–35.
2. Rom. 14:12.
3. Heb. 4:13.

Chapter Three
Heaven's Purpose: Transforming Our Image

1. Rom. 6:3, 6.
2. Rom. 6:5.
3. Col. 3:1–3.
4. Matt. 22:2–14.
5. Col. 3:12.
6. Rom. 13:14.
7. Col. 3:9–10.
8. Gen. 3:7.
9. See Col. 2:20–23; 2 Tim. 3:1–5.
10. Gen. 3:9.
11. See Eph. 4:20–24.
12. Isa. 64:6.
13. Heb. 4:12.

Chapter Four
Heaven's Call: Wholehearted Obedience

1. Matt. 19:16–24.
2. Matt. 6:20–21.

3. Matt. 6:24.
4. Rom. 6:17.
5. Matt. 16:23.
6. See Matt. 3:8; Acts 26:20; 2 Cor. 7:8–11.
7. See Luke 6:27–36; John 14:27.
8. John 7:24.
9. See Phil. 1:9–11; Eph. 5:9–11; Matt. 7:15–23.
10. Matt. 12:34.
11. Heb. 13:15.
12. See Matt. 12:33–37; James 3:1–18.
13. Rom. 15:23–28.
14. See Acts 20:35; Heb. 10:34; 2 Cor. 8–9.
15. John 4:34–38.
16. See Rom. 15:28; Heb. 13:15; Phil. 1:11; Matt. 3:8.
17. See Rom. 5:6–11.
18. Matt. 13.
19. Ps. 85:7–8, 10–11.

PART TWO
Imitating Heaven's Model:
Impact through Discipleship

Prelude

1. John 1:1, 14.
2. Col. 2:9–10.
3. Eph. 1:22–23.
4. Eph. 5:1–2.
5. John 13:15.
6. 1 Pet. 2:21.

Chapter Five
Imitating Heaven's Touch: Becoming the Hands of Heaven

1. Matt. 17:6–8.
2. Luke 7:11–17.

Chapter Six
Imitating Heaven's Look: Reflecting the Eyes of Heaven

1. Luke 8:47.
2. See Matt. 18:12.
3. See Luke 18:9.
4. See Matt. 18:10.
5. Luke 16:15.
6. See Matt. 6:1–4.
7. Col. 3:12.
8. Luke 11:33–35.
9. 2 Cor. 4:18.
10. Luke 19:10.
11. John 4:4–42.
12. John 4:35.
13. John 5:41–44.
14. Luke 15.
15. Luke 15:20.
16. Steven Curtis Chapman and Geoff Moore, "If You Could See What I See" (Sparrow Song/Peach Hill Songs/Star STruck Music Admin. by EMI Christian Music Publishing, 1993).

Chapter Seven
Imitating Heaven's Voice: Sharing the Word of Heaven

1. See Matt. 12:34; James 3.
2. Ps. 17:3.
3. Ps. 19:14.
4. Prov. 16:23.
5. Matt. 8:3.
6. Matt. 8:7.
7. Matt. 9:2.
8. Matt. 9:13.
9. Matt. 11:28.
10. Matt. 14:27.
11. Matt. 20:28.
12. Matt. 20:32.
13. Matt. 26:10.

14. Matt. 26:42.
15. Matt. 10:29.
16. Luke 15:32.
17. Luke 22:32.
18. Luke 23:34.
19. John 8:11.
20. John 15:15.
21. John 20:16.
22. John 20:21.
23. John 21:12.
24. James 3:8.
25. See James 3:1–12; Matt. 12:36–37; 2 Tim. 2:23–26.
26. Eph. 5:4, 6–7.
27. Col. 4:6.
28. Col. 4:29.
29. Eph. 4:15.
30. Matt. 23:13–15, 23–24.

Chapter Eight
Imitating Heaven's Heart: Demonstrating the Heart of Heaven

1. Col. 3:1.
2. Stewart Hample and Eric Marshall, comp., *Children's Letters to God* (New York: Workman Publishing, 1991).
3. Matt. 23:23.
4. Luke 11:42.
5. Matt. 7:12.
6. Matt. 22:37–40.
7. Mark 12:30–31.
8. Rom. 13:9b–10.
9. Gal. 5:14.
10. Alan Loy McGinnis "The Power of Optimism," in *Chicken Soup for the Soul,* by Jack Canfield and Mark Victor Hansen (Health Communications, Inc.), 266.
11. Steve Hillage and Miquette Giraudy, "Fire Inside," Bob Seger (EMI Virgin Music, Ltd., 1979).

PART THREE
Embracing Heaven's Methods:
Maturity through Hardship

Prelude
1. Mark 9:24.

Chapter Nine
Maturing through Pain: Committing When You Feel Like Quitting

1. Exod. 19:3–8, 10–11.
2. Exod. 32:7–10.
3. Ephraim is one of the twelve tribe/states of Israel and is used as a name for the nation.
4. Admah and Zeboiim were suburbs of Sodom and Gomorrah and were destroyed with them.
5. Exod. 32:25–26.
6. Exod. 32:27–35.
7. Exod. 33:12–14, 19; 34:6–10.
8. Luke 23:32–34
9. Mark 15:29–32
10. Luke 23:39–43.

Chapter Ten
Maturing through Testing: Standing Firm When You Feel Blown Away

1. James 1:2–4.
2. Gen. 22:1–2.
3. Heb. 11:12; Rom. 4:18–19.
4. Rev. 11:15.
5. Matt. 4:10.
6. See Rom. 12:1–2.
7. Ezek. 18:32.

8. James 1:13.
9. See Mal. 2:16.
10. Gen. 22:3.
11. See Rom. 4:18–21.
12. Gen. 22:9–12.
13. Gen. 22:13.
14. Gen. 22:14–18.
15. Eph. 3:20–21.
16. Phil. 4:13.
17. 2 Cor. 12:8–10.
18. 2 Tim. 4:16–18.

Chapter Eleven
Maturing through Confrontation: Receiving Rebuke When You Want to Return Fire

1. See 1 Kings 18:16–39.
2. 1 Kings 18:15–18.
3. Prov. 27:17.
4. Heb. 10:24.
5. Matt. 6:24; Luke 16:13; 9:62; Mark 9:40.
6. 1 Kings 18:26b.
7. 1 Kings 18:27–29.
8. 1 Kings 18:39.
9. 1 Kings 18:37.
10. Heb. 12:11.
11. Eph. 6:12
12. 2 Cor. 10:3–5.
13. 1 Cor. 11:32.

Chapter Twelve
Maturing through Pain: Reaching Out When You Feel Like Reeling In

1. Phil. 2:5–7.
2. Bill Hybels, *Descending into Greatness* (Grand Rapids, Mich.: Zondervan Publishing House, 1993).

3. Acts 7:23–25.
4. Acts 7:26–28.
5. Exod. 2:14–15.
6. Exod. 3:1.
7. Exod. 3:2–4.
8. Exod. 3:5–8.
9. Exod. 3:10.
10. Exod. 3:11.
11. Ibid.
12. Exod. 3:13.
13. Exod. 4:1.
14. Exod. 4:10.
15. Exod. 4:13.
16. Acts 7:35.
17. Exod. 3:12.
18. Rom. 8:31.
19. Heb. 13:5.
20. Matt. 28:20.
21. 1 Kings 19:4.
22. 1 Kings 19:10.
23. 1 Kings 19:11.
24. 1 Kings 19:11–13.
25. 1 Kings 19:18.
26. Luke 9:28–31.
27. Deut. 1:6–7.
28. 1 John 3:16–19.
29. Acts 14:22.
30. Phil. 1:6.
31. Steven Curtis Chapman and Geoff Moore, "The Mountain" (Sparrow Song/Peach Hill Songs/Starstruck Music Admin. by EMI Christian Music Publishing, 1994).

Conclusion
God's Pledge Of Allegiance

1. Heb. 12:2–5, 7, 11.
2. Rom. 12:1–2.
3. Col. 3:1–4.